PARENTING KIDS WITH ADHD

Unlock Focus, Boost Confidence, and Spark Joy with 10 Quick and Easy Strategies to Harness ADHD as a Superpower

Phoenix J. Waldren

Copyright 2024 - All rights reserved.

All rights reserved. No part of this guide may be reproduced, transmitted, or distributed in any form or by any means without permission in writing from the publisher except in the case of brief quotations embodied in critical articles or reviews.

Legal & Disclaimer

The content and information in this book are consistent and truthful, and it has been provided for informational, educational, and business purposes only.

TABLE OF CONTENTS

Introduction 5
    Understanding the Basis 8

Chapter One 14
    Unveiling the Superpower - A New Perspective on ADHD 14
        Understanding ADHD Beyond the Myths 15
        Key Takeaways 33

Chapter Two 35
    Discovering Your Child's Learning Superpower 35
        The Spectrum of Learning Styles 36
        The Role of Technology in Adaptive Learning 42
        Key Takeaways 54

Chapter Three 55
    The Mastery of Impulse-Guiding Self-Control 55
        Recognizing triggers and patterns of impulsive behavior 57
        Strategies for Self-Regulation 62
        Key Takeaways 75

Chapter Four 77
    The Social Maze - Navigating Friendships with and without ADHD ... 77
        Friendships with Peers with ADHD 84
        Key Takeaways 93

Chapter Five 95
    Emotional Superheroes - Harnessing Emotional Intelligence 95
        Why is EQ so important for kids with ADHD? 96
        How to Create an Emotionally Intelligent Household 108
        Key Takeaways 117

Chapter Six 121

Hyper-Focus: The Secret Lair of Concentration *121*
    Channeling Hyper-Focus Productively 123
    Positive Impact of Hyper-Focus 131
    Key Takeaways 139

Chapter Seven **141**
  The Rhythm of Routine – Structuring Success for ADHD Minds *141*
    The Key Elements of a Successful Routine 152
    Key Takeaways 163

Chapter Eight **164**
  Fueling a Superheroes Fire – Nutrition and Exercise for the ADHD Brain *164*
    Supplements and ADHD 177
    The Exercise-ADHD Connection 180
    Mind-Body Practices 182
    Key Takeaways 190

Chapter Nine **192**
  Allies in Action - Advocating for ADHD in Education and Beyond *192*
    Understanding your Child's Rights 195
    Strategies for Effective Advocacy 196
    Key Takeaways 205

Chapter Ten **207**
  The Symphony of Support - Building a community *207*
    The Value of a Strong Support Network 208
    How to Build and Maintain a Support Network 211
    Inclusivity and Advocacy 217
    Key Takeaways 221

Conclusion **223**

Reflecting on the Journey **224**

References **235**

Introduction

"You're going to get a lot of advice from people, and you can take bits and pieces, but you know innately what your child needs. It would help if you trusted that. Don't beat yourself up for making decisions about things that may or may not work. It's an experiment, and you're a part of that."

– **Lucy Liu**

Now, it is no longer news. The doctor has confirmed your child is struggling with ADHD, and that helps clear your doubt. But how did you feel? Guilty or perplexed? Indifferent, worried, frustrated, or confused? Your answer means a lot to me. Do you know why? I have been there, and so are the parents of over 6 million children with ADHD in America. Were you bothered or confused when the doctor told you? I can imagine how you feel. Maybe you have noticed the symptoms for a while, but you just needed to confirm. Still, in all, the feelings are almost always the same: frustration, confusion, and something in between. Most parents always feel frustrated or confused, unclear about the cause and the next step to take.

No matter how long your child has been living with this condition or how recently they received a diagnosis, as parents, we always experience similar emotions. As you may have experienced, I too felt frustrated upon receiving my child's diagnosis. I thought of a million things within a second, yet I couldn't wrap my head around one. I asked the doctor many questions until my appointment time was up that day. Yet, I didn't feel satisfied or fulfilled. Not because he wasn't saying anything meaningful, but because I was so confused. I hit the internet. Yet, I couldn't get any answer that could put my mind at rest. I wanted some form of solution that could help address my child's struggle with these symptoms. I wanted some medicine. You know, just a pill or a line of treatment or training for the child, but after a while, I realized that all my child needs is me.

Contrary to the first attempt, which is medicine or training for children that is common among parents, I realized something. It wasn't the child who required training or a quick-fix medication; it was me who required instruction on how to offer support and encouragement.

So, I had no option but to start the journey. I tapped into my child's unknown world and explored different possibilities in a way I never had before. Well, that takes the whole of me, myself, and I fully meshed into my child's world, but after many years, I have a different story to tell, a positive one at that. How I got the victory and strategies to help are what necessitated this book.

The journey of raising a child with ADHD is challenging, but I have learned that it can be easy with effective parenting strategies. It doesn't matter if your child has recently received a diagnosis or has been managing this condition for some time. You don't need to think about many things. That may make you more bothered. But be rest assured that you can raise a child with ADHD to a full-grown superstar like I did without losing your mind, as so many parents think.

Understanding the Basis

Perhaps you are thinking, or you've been told, that ADHD is a disease. I want you to dispel that thought. ADHD is far from it. First, you need to know that the brain makes the difference. I don't want to bore you with too much jargon or medical terms about this disorder. However, I simply want you to know that your child is not suffering from a sickness; rather, they are suffering from a disorder. When I say disorder, it is not something too difficult to understand. Your child is struggling with attentional regulation. This simply means they are paying attention to too many things, and because of that, it becomes hard to always direct attention to a priority.

Have you observed that sometimes, if you ask your child to help out with something at home, it takes more time than usual? It may seem to you like they always lose something, fidget or talk constantly, don't listen to (or want to do) what you say, and can't stay concentrated. Plus, have you noticed that sometimes your child takes risks that are unsafe for others and themselves? As a parent, it's not always easy to keep up with, much less stay one step ahead of a kid like this.

I often like to tell parents that nothing is wrong with their children when they are diagnosed. Paying attention and staying focused on something, whether in the classroom or at home, might require extra effort. And expecting a kid with ADHD (attention-deficit/hyperactivity disorder) to sit and sustain is like asking your left-handed child to handwrite an essay using the right hand. That's not impossible, but it would require extra effort, and they may likely give up in frustration.

This means the skills that control behaviors, activity, and attention don't come naturally to your kids. Understanding the way the ADHD brain tends to function, as well as how your particular child's brain works, can help you empathize with their struggles and make you ready to give support and encouragement to complement different strategies and techniques alongside the pills to address the challenges they face.

Tapping into Your Child's World

So, let me ask you:

Do you know all that your child needs from you?

Whether your child has received a recent diagnosis or has been coping with the condition for some time, your readiness to provide support and encouragement is crucial. It is not enough to know your child is struggling with ADHD. What's more important is knowing where you can help as a parent. I don't want you to get me wrong; I just want you to know that knowing your child's ADHD status is the first and simple step. It helps clear doubt, as I have said earlier. Maybe you thought your child was purposefully ignoring your instructions or trying to cause difficulty. But now you have a clearer picture. However, you don't know. More so, it is not about using pills or a line of treatment. It is about being willing to provide the support.

As a parent of a child with ADHD, it is important that you know that you set the stage for your child's physical and emotional health. Let me tell you this explicitly: no one truly cares for your child as much as you do. Having that understanding makes you know you are all your child has. They're the best friends of all time. So, you just have to pay a little more attention than you would to other children.

It is not easy to parent a child with ADHD. When the child misbehaves, strangers can feel justified in offering advice or commenting about your parenting choice. Even family and friends may criticize your parenting style. But giving full attention helps you figure out your child's needs and explain to others why your child is different. It enables you to know when and where to come in. Even though some people share their pain and show some concern, your support and encouragement are too necessary to be ignored. So, let me tell you, just as I have been telling thousands of parents, I have said that as a parent, you set the stage for your child's emotional and physical health. In other words, your position is more than just being a parent; it is that of a love-giver, encourager, and supporter. That is why I often tell parents that their best assets for helping their child cope with the symptoms of ADHD are their positive attitudes and common sense. A little effort to bring out the hidden 'Them".

I know dealing with this condition can be so frustrating, right? Of course, I know. Sometimes, you are just embarrassed about what other people think of your child's behavior. Imagine a bustling classroom with pupils absorbed in their work and your child trying to remain seated, their thoughts rushing ahead like a speeding train. Sometimes, you just can't help but wish for a miracle. Other times, you yell or shout at your child for their inability to cope with others. Such feelings are real, but it is best if you see this time as an avenue to start a trip to discover your child's uniqueness. That your child can't cope with math or pass basic science doesn't mean they won't excel in other spheres different from academics.

When their children receive an ADHD diagnosis, parents often feel guilty and wonder if they have done something wrong. But over time, those who truly want to be supportive learn to accept the reality that they have to raise and nurture superheroes with special needs and attention. So, it moves from what they feel to how ready they are to take up the task. So, let me ask you, "Are you ready?" or better still, "How ready are you to empathize with your child's struggles and help them through them without definite solutions?"

My Motivation

Over the years, I have learned the weaknesses, strengths, and something in between; that is why I wrote this book to share. Some secrets with you and thousands of other parents of children with ADHD. I know that what most parents are searching for at this point is the solution. Or perhaps how to cope or give the best support ever. But if you ask me? The first solution is THEM. Being willing to tap into their child's world and provide support is what makes the difference.

You see, I write this book to share some secrets you possibly won't see anywhere. I want you to know that the difference between non-ADHD children and children with ADHD is in the support given by the parents and whatever constitutes their environment, school, teachers, or what they have. This book delves into what you should expect when your child is struggling with an inattentive or impulsive disorder and how you can be of help. You will read some probable causes or risk factors reasons why your child is facing this challenge. You will learn to correctly instruct and guide your child when things become overwhelming.

Let's get started!

Chapter One

Unveiling the Superpower - A New Perspective on ADHD

"With great power comes great responsibility."

– Spider-Man (Peter Parker)

Do you know Michael Phelps? A former American competitive swimmer, considered the most decorated Olympian of all time. He has a record of twenty-eight medals—twenty-three gold, three silver, and two bronze medals. That's incredible, right? What if I told you that he has ADHD and that his success story would be incomplete without acknowledging how ADHD contributes to his remarkable achievements?

Just like many children, he had attention difficulties and behavior problems at school. But he didn't allow that to stop. him. It was his superpower that helped him become an icon in the Olympics. Michael Phelps said that he found swimming to be the perfect outlet for his hyperactivity. From that moment, he maximized every moment in the waters and became a famous gold medalist swimmer.

Why did I tell you about Michael Phelps? So that you know that a child with ADHD is not limited, ADHD can be a superpower that will propel them to unimaginable heights of greatness. To be honest, a lot of lies have been said about ADHD. They have pushed wrong narratives about the disorder that makes most parents troubled when they know their children have it. The truth is that ADHD is not what many people think it is. In this chapter, we will be breaking many walls of lies and making you see new perspectives about ADHD. Let's dive in.

Understanding ADHD Beyond the Myths

People often paint vivid pictures of ADHD. Typically, a restless child bouncing off the walls, unable to focus or sit still. While there is some truth in this stereotype for some individuals with ADHD, it paints an incomplete and often inaccurate picture of this complex neurodevelopmental disorder. In this section, we move beyond the myths and misconceptions that surround ADHD and have a deeper understanding of its diverse spectrum and the unique strengths it can offer.

Myth 1: ADHD is a "fake" condition.

This harmful misconception often stems from a lack of understanding about the brain and its workings. ADHD isn't a figment of imagination or a character flaw; it's a real, biologically-based condition with identifiable differences in brain activity. Neurotransmitter imbalances, particularly in dopamine and norepinephrine, which play crucial roles in attention, focus, and impulse control, can cause it.

Myth 2: Bad parenting or a lack of discipline leads to ADHD.

Attributing ADHD to parenting styles is not only insensitive, but also factually incorrect. There is no evidence linking parenting to the development of ADHD. This myth can be incredibly damaging to families, placing undue blame and shame where it doesn't belong.

Myth 3: ADHD is just about being hyperactive and fidgety.

While hyperactivity and impulsivity are often associated with ADHD, they are not the only symptoms, and not everyone with ADHD experiences them to the same degree. "Predominantly inattentive" ADHD is a subtype that is characterized by difficulty focusing, easily becoming distracted, and losing track of things. Many individuals with ADHD also struggle with executive functioning skills, such as planning, organizing, and managing time.

Myth 4: People with ADHD can't focus on anything.

This is another harmful generalization that ignores the unique strengths of individuals with ADHD. While they might struggle with sustained attention in traditional settings, they can often hyper-focus on activities that they find engaging or stimulating. This can translate to exceptional creativity, passion, and dedication in their chosen pursuits.

Myth 5: ADHD is a disease that needs to be cured.

ADHD is a unique way of processing information and experiencing the world, not a disease that requires cure. It's important to shift the narrative from fixing or curing ADHD to embracing it as a unique trait with both challenges and advantages. When viewed through this lens, individuals with ADHD can focus on developing their strengths, finding supportive communities, and celebrating their neurodiversity.

Myth 6: People with ADHD are lazy or unintelligent.

This myth couldn't be further from the truth. Many individuals with ADHD are highly intelligent, creative, and accomplished. Challenges with attention and organization don't equate to a lack of intelligence or motivation.

Moving beyond these misconceptions is crucial not only for creating a more inclusive and understanding environment for individuals with ADHD but also for recognizing their unique strengths and potential. By embracing the diversity of ADHD experiences, we can celebrate the individuals who defy stereotypes and achieve greatness, just as Michael Phelps did, fueled by his unique superpower.

Exploring the Neuroscientific Basis of ADHD

Now that we have broken down the walls of falsehood about ADHD, let's go on to explore the neuroscientific basis of ADHD. This will help you gain deeper insight into how someone with ADHD behaves in certain ways. Complex neurobiological mechanisms that influence cognitive functions and behavior is the root cause of ADHD. To be honest, one cannot say the exact cause of ADHD, but scientific research has shed light on how diverse structures and functions of the nervous system play a role in ADHD. Let's proceed.

The Frontal Lobe:

The frontal lobe performs executive functions like focus, planning, and organization. In ADHD brains, the prefrontal cortex, which is the brain's control center within the frontal lobe, can be underdeveloped. This can lead to difficulties with attention, working memory, and impulse control.

Basal Ganglia:

Think of the basal ganglia as the brain's communication hub, connecting different regions and ensuring smooth coordination. In ADHD, this hub might have fewer connections, impacting the flow of information and potentially explaining why some individuals struggle with multitasking or switching between tasks.

The Limbic System:

The limbic system, the brain's emotional control center, also plays a role in ADHD. Certain areas within this system might have reduced white matter integrity, potentially impacting learning, memory, and regulating emotions. This could explain why some people with ADHD experience difficulties managing emotions or staying motivated.

Corpus Callosum:

The corpus callosum, the bridge connecting the brain's left and right hemispheres, might also have structural differences in ADHD brains. This can hinder communication between the hemispheres, potentially contributing to attention difficulties and processing challenges.

Neurotransmitters:

Dopamine, the brain's reward system chemical, plays a crucial role in motivation, focus, and pleasure. In ADHD brains, there might be an imbalance in dopamine levels or receptors, leading to difficulties in experiencing rewards and staying motivated. This could be the reason why some individuals with ADHD seek out intense experiences to compensate for the lack of natural reward. Also, individuals with ADHD might have variations in the norepinephrine (a neurotransmitter that helps regulate stress and attention) transporter gene, potentially impacting their stress response and attention span.

While neuroscientists don't have the whole picture yet, these findings paint a portrait of the brain in ADHD. It's not just about a single region or chemical; it's a complex interplay of various structures and neurotransmitters. By understanding this interplay, we can move beyond misconceptions and develop effective strategies to support individuals with ADHD and unlock their full potential.

The Evolutionary Advantages of ADHD Traits

Attention Deficit Hyperactivity Disorder often carries the stigma of dysfunction in a classroom setting. But what if those very traits—impulsive bursts, insatiable curiosity, the laser focus on novelty—were once adaptive tools honed during the harsh realities of our nomadic ancestors? Imagine a nomadic world where survival depends on quick reflexes, resourcefulness, and adaptability. ADHD traits might not have been a hindrance but a hidden advantage.

Hyper-focus: The ability to laser in on a task, ignoring distractions, could have been crucial for tracking prey, crafting tools, or navigating treacherous terrain.

Impulsivity: Acting quickly in the face of danger, such as a sabertoothed tiger on the prowl or a sudden flash flood, could have meant the difference between life and death.

Novelty-seeking: Exploring new environments and trying new approaches could have led to the discovery of new food sources, safer routes, or advantageous hunting grounds.

Creativity: unconventional thinking and problem-solving skills could have been essential for crafting innovative tools, adapting to changing environments, and finding solutions in the face of limited resources.

Now, instead of viewing ADHD solely as a disability, we can start to appreciate it as a different way of processing information and navigating the world. The strengths associated with ADHD, like creativity, resourcefulness, and adaptability, can flourish in the right environment. By recognizing the potential evolutionary advantages of ADHD traits, we can shift the narrative from deficit to diversity. We can create educational and professional environments that embrace these strengths and allow individuals with ADHD to thrive.

ADHD in the Real World

Imagine a world where people with ADHD aren't just seen as fidgety and forgetful but as talented artists, successful entrepreneurs, and even Olympic champions. That's the real story of ADHD!

Contrary to the perception of ADHD as a barrier to achievement, statistics paint a different picture. Individuals with ADHD are well-represented across various fields, achieving remarkable success. In entrepreneurship, Richard Branson, founder of Virgin Group, and Jeff Bezos, the mastermind behind Amazon, both identify with ADHD. In the creative sphere, actors like Will Smith and Channing Tatum and athletes like Michael Phelps have harnessed their ADHD traits to fuel their artistry. These are just a few examples of the countless individuals who have defied the stereotypical limitations associated with ADHD.

The Relationship between ADHD, Creativity, and the Environment. The link between ADHD and creativity is undeniable. The traits often associated with ADHD, such as hyper-focus, divergent thinking, and a heightened sense of novelty, can be the fuel for remarkable creative expression. The ability to hyper-focus on a passion project, to see connections where others see walls, and to constantly seek new ideas—these are the hallmarks of a creative mind. Individuals with ADHD often possess an innate ability to think creatively, challenge assumptions, and generate innovative solutions. This makes them valuable assets in fields that require ingenuity and imagination, from art and design to science and technology.

While ADHD presents unique challenges, the environment plays a crucial role in shaping outcomes. A supportive and understanding environment can be the difference between thriving and struggling. Educational settings that cater to the diverse learning styles of individuals with ADHD can unlock their potential. Workplaces that recognize and value their strengths can create a space where they can excel. Understanding and acceptance, both from individuals and society as a whole, are key to fostering a sense of belonging and empowerment for those with ADHD.

Embracing the ADHD Identity

ADHD is not a disease; it's a different way of processing information and experiencing the world. Instead of viewing it solely as a diagnosis, embracing its unique identity is important. Individuals with ADHD possess many strengths, including resilience, adaptability, resourcefulness, and, yes, even a touch of chaos – that can be channeled into positive forces. By celebrating these strengths, building upon them, and finding supportive communities, individuals with ADHD can thrive in the real world.

Encouraging a Positive Self-image in Children with ADHD

Nurturing a positive self-image in children with ADHD is crucial. Emphasize their distinctive strengths such as creativity, energy, and spontaneity. Create supportive environments where these qualities can thrive. Teach resilience and adaptive problem-solving, transforming obstacles into opportunities. Regularly celebrate small achievements and reinforce that differences do not dictate value. By cultivating self-acceptance and empathy, we empower these children to transcend their challenges and confidently embrace their vast potential.

- **Help children with ADHD Process Feelings:**

Attention Deficit Hyperactivity Disorder isn't just about scattered attention; it can also affect how young people experience and express emotions. When faced with challenging situations, especially transitions or new expectations, their emotions might feel like raging rapids, difficult to navigate alone. This is where supportive adults, like teachers and parents, become crucial guides.

Instead of labeling the behavior as inherently "bad," focus on understanding the underlying reasons. Was it a late night that left them cranky? Could hunger be fueling their frustration? Did that extended period of focus without a break trigger hyperactivity? By exploring these possibilities, you can help them healthily unpack their emotional baggage.

- **Remind children of their positive behavior:**

ADHD is often associated with challenges, sometimes overshadowing the incredible strengths these children possess. By reminding them of their positive qualities, we can help build their self-image and empower them to confidently navigate life's challenges.

One powerful strategy is creating a "sunshine list." This is a personal inventory of their unique strengths and talents. Place this list in a visible location, such as near their desk or on the fridge, to remind them of their inherent goodness.

You can write about those times they tackled a project with focus or surprised everyone with their creative spark. Mention how their energy motivates and inspires others. You can also recall moments where they showed concern for others, offered a helping hand, or stood up for what they believed in.

- **Allow them to discover their strength:**

The traditional one-size-fits-all approach to learning might not spark the hidden potential of children with ADHD. What they need is the freedom to experiment, explore, and stumble upon their unique strengths. Some children with ADHD can channel their inherent "risk-taking" into problem-solving. Their out-of-the-box thinking can crack open complex challenges, leading to innovative solutions and groundbreaking ideas. This can be a significant asset in fields like science, math, or any sphere that thrives on fresh ideas.

- **Create room for success:**

Success can lead to motivation, fuel positive learning attitudes, and influence performance, especially for children with ADHD. But how do we create room for success?

Imagine a child struggling to read a long passage. Breaking it down into smaller, more manageable paragraphs makes it easier. Each paragraph read, each comprehension exercise mastered, is a victory. These' mini-adventures' in understanding not only strengthen focus and reading skills but also enhance their confidence, making the next paragraph seem less daunting.

Similarly, for students grappling with challenges in handwriting, introducing an engaging typing program can be beneficial. This not only helps in developing keyboarding skills but also allows students to experience success, contributing to increased confidence in writing activities.

Strategies for Discussing ADHD with Your Child

When you have a child with ADHD, it is important to talk to them about it. They need to know why they are unique. I know it might be a bit challenging, but the following tips will help you navigate the process of discussing ADHD with your child.

- **Start with a Foundation of Love and Acceptance:**

    Before diving into discussions about ADHD, create a space of unconditional love and acceptance. Let your child know you care for them deeply, no matter what. Remind them that you believe in their intelligence and abilities, and that ADHD doesn't define them. It's simply a different way their brain works, just like some people have different colored eyes or wear glasses to see better. You can say something like, "No matter what we learn about ADHD, remember you're always my awesome kid, full of potential, and loved every step of the way."

    This shift in focus prioritizes your child's emotional well-being and sets the stage for a positive and constructive conversation about ADHD. Remember, feeling loved and accepted is crucial for any child, especially when addressing challenges like ADHD.

- **Choose the Moment wisely:**

Timing is everything, especially when approaching a sensitive topic like ADHD. Opt for a calm, uninterrupted environment where you can connect without distractions. Avoid moments when your child's attention is elsewhere, like during playtime, right before dinner, or close to bedtime. Instead, choose a quiet time where you can both be fully present and engage in a thoughtful conversation.

Remember, this isn't a one-and-done talk. Leave ample time for follow-up questions and open-ended discussion. Your child might need time to process the information or have additional concerns they want to share. Being available and accessible after the initial conversation shows your dedication to supporting them through this journey.

- **Let them know they are not alone:**

    Remember, your child isn't on this journey alone. Let them know that ADHD affects millions of people, including some of the most successful individuals in the world. Walt Disney's imagination took flight with ADHD, and Michael Phelps conquered Olympic pools with his laser focus. These inspirational examples can empower your child to see ADHD not as a limitation but as a unique characteristic that can fuel exceptional achievements.

    Consider connecting your child with someone they admire who also has ADHD. A relatable conversation with a cousin, family friend, or even a mentor can make a big difference. Hearing from someone who shares their experience can normalize their challenges and offer valuable insights and tips.

- **Don't be in haste:**

    When discussing ADHD with your child, remember that their response might not bloom instantly. If they appear uninterested or hesitant to engage right away, don't let it discourage you. Processing new information and formulating questions takes time, especially for younger children.

Think of it as planting a seed. The first conversation is just the first step. The information you share needs time to germinate and take root in their understanding. Some children might absorb it quickly, while others might need space to ponder, mull it over, and connect it to their own experiences.

- **Don't use ADHD as an excuse:**

While discussing ADHD, it's important to avoid framing it solely as a reason for setbacks or limitations. Instead, let's shift the focus towards empowering your child to understand and manage their challenges. ADHD shouldn't be an excuse for avoiding responsibilities or giving up. When faced with a setback, work together to identify solutions instead of dwelling on why things went wrong. Identify strategies and techniques that can assist them in navigating similar situations in the future.

In conclusion, we have explored the multifaceted nature of ADHD, challenging the prevailing notion of it as a limitation and instead presenting it as a potential superpower when approached positively. Just as icons like Michael Phelps have demonstrated, individuals with ADHD possess unique strengths that can lead to remarkable success. Recognizing and embracing these strengths can be transformative for the children under our care.

In the next chapter, we will delve into unique learning styles tailored to children with ADHD. By understanding and accommodating these specific needs, we pave the way for a future where these children not only overcome challenges but also emerge as confident, capable adults.

Key Takeaways

- ADHD can be a superpower, as seen in Michael Phelps.

- Myths about ADHD include ADHD as a fake condition, blaming parenting, and the misconception that people with ADHD can't focus on anything.

- ADHD is marked by underdeveloped frontal lobes, fewer connections in the basal ganglia, effects on the limbic system, differences in the structure of the corpus callosum, and an imbalance of neurotransmitters.

- Many successful people with ADHD, such as Richard Branson and Michael Phelps, challenge the idea that ADHD limits achievement.

- Strategies for children with ADHD include emotional support, recognizing strengths, allowing self-discovery, creating room for success, and effective communication.

- Discussing ADHD with children involves starting with love and acceptance, choosing the right moment, emphasizing they are not alone, being patient, and avoiding using ADHD as an excuse.

Chapter Two

Discovering Your Child's Learning Superpower

"I've been fighting with one arm tied behind my back but what happens when I'm finally set free."

- Captain Marvel.

What if your child's learning style is their greatest asset? Imagine that your child's love for moving around isn't a distraction but a secret key to academic success. Imagine that their endless energy isn't a problem but a superpower that helps them come up with creative ideas. What if the way your child learns, which might seem a bit different, is the key to unlocking their amazing potential?

That's why it's crucial to learn more about diverse learning styles and discover how to understand your child's unique learning style. This approach can ignite their passion for learning and unleash their hidden abilities. It's not just about knowing there are different ways to learn; it's about welcoming them as the guide that helps your child move towards a successful future. Let's proceed.

The Spectrum of Learning Styles

There are different types of learning styles for kids. Presently, there are seven (7) known learning styles, each unique to different children. Below are some learning styles that may be suitable for your child with ADHD:

- **Solitary or Intrapersonal:**

    Children with a solitary learning style prefer working independently. They thrive in environments where they can focus on individual tasks, avoiding distractions from others. Solitary learners often excel in self-directed activities, allowing them to examine their thoughts and processes.

- **Social or Interpersonal:**

    This learning style thrives on social interaction and group dynamics. Children with a social preference enjoy collaborative projects, group discussions, and learning activities that involve teamwork. They tend to absorb information effectively through interaction and communication with peers, making group settings conducive to their academic success.

- **Logical or Mathematical:**

    Logical or mathematical learners rely on systems, reasoning, and logic to understand and retain information. These children excel in subjects that involve patterns, critical thinking, and problem-solving. They are analytical thinkers who appreciate structure and order in their learning experiences, often thriving in environments where they can apply logical processes to grasp complex concepts.

- **Physical or Kinesthetic:**

    Children with a physical or kinesthetic learning style thrive when actively engaging their body and sense of touch in the learning process. Movement, hands-on activities, and physical experiences enhance their understanding and retention of information. This style is notably common among children with ADHD and other learning disabilities.

- **Verbal or Linguistic:**

    Verbal or linguistic learning styles involve a preference for written and spoken words. Children with this style excel in reading, writing, speaking, and listening activities. They learn best through discussions, written materials, and verbal explanations, making language-rich environments conducive to their academic growth.

- **Aural or Auditory-Musical:**

    Aural or auditory-musical learners favor using sound, music, and rhythm as key elements in their learning process. These children absorb information effectively through auditory cues, such as spoken instructions, discussions, and musical elements. Incorporating music or auditory aids enhances their learning experiences.

- **Visual or Spatial:**

    Children with a visual or spatial learning style excel in understanding information through images, spatial relationships, and visual aids. They prefer using charts, diagrams, and other visual materials to grasp concepts. Environments that present information visually enhance the comprehension and retention of knowledge for visual or spatial learners.

So, the question is, how do you know the learning style that is suitable for your child?

The truth is that every child is unique, and as a result, they will have a distinctive preferred method of understanding. Simply because a particular approach proves effective for one child with ADHD doesn't guarantee that it will work for all children. Therefore, the most effective strategy involves experimentation with various learning styles. It is essential to navigate through these options until you identify the one, or potentially more than one, that resonates best with your child. In teaching children with ADHD, the absence of a singular correct method allows for flexibility. The key lies in discerning what the child comprehends and finds most comfortable and subsequently adapting the learning process accordingly.

> *"Heroes are made by the path they choose, not the powers they are graced with." - **Iron Man (Tony Stark)***

Tailoring Education to Your Child's ADHD Profile

If you have a child with ADHD, here are ways you can tailor your child's education to meet their profile.

- **Give clear and structured instructions:**

    One fantastic approach to tailoring education to your child's ADHD profile is giving clear and structured instructions. Having a routine is golden. You can start the day by laying out what's on the agenda. Visual schedules with colorful illustrations work wonders. You can display them where your child can't miss them. Predictability helps ease any anxiety and makes the day more manageable.

Additionally, since effective communication is crucial, it's crucial to establish unambiguous expectations. Whether it's group work behavior or nailing down the specifics of an assignment, keep it simple. Furthermore, visuals like diagrams, charts, and pictures can help your child grasp new ideas and remember stuff better. For those multi-step tasks, a visual step-by-step guide can be a game-changer. It not only keeps them on track, but it also helps them prepare for what's coming next.

Checklists and planners can also help them stay organized. Break down bigger projects into bite-sized chunks with a checklist. Planners—daily or weekly — are fantastic for mapping out tasks and homework. And for the younger ones, a homework folder keeps everything in one place, reducing the chances of lost assignments.

So, by making things clear and structured, we're not just helping them with schoolwork. We're also giving them skills that will be handy in everyday life.

- **Utilize multi-sensory learning:**

    Multi-sensory learning provides better focus, understanding, and memory. You can consider using visuals like charts, diagrams, or anything colorful and eye-catching. This helps your child connect the dots between different bits of knowledge. Also, you can maximize the use of sounds. Reading aloud, catchy songs or educational podcasts will not only make learning fun but also help with understanding and remembering. In addition, encouraging your child to share their thoughts out loud can be a memory booster.

That's not all. Kinesthetic activities like hands-on experiments, math with manipulatives, or acting out scenes in a story get your child physically involved. It's like learning while jumping rope or doing a little dance. By incorporating multi-sensory learning, you can turn learning into a dynamic, exciting adventure for kids with ADHD.

The Role of Technology in Adaptive Learning

Adaptive learning transforms the traditional classroom into a personalized experience for each student. In this system, technology acts as a guide to understanding your child's strengths and weaknesses through smart algorithms and data analysis. It adapts to their learning style, utilizing interactive games, videos, or explanations. Rather than a one-size-fits-all approach, adaptive learning creates individualized roadmaps for students to adjust to as they progress. It offers instant feedback and provides support when needed, turning learning into an engaging adventure.

However, it's important to note that technology is a tool, not a replacement. Teachers and parents remain the true heroes, using insights from adaptive learning to tailor guidance to individual needs. This collaboration ensures a supportive and enriching learning environment where technology complements, rather than replaces, human connection.

So, consider how technology can bridge the gap to a brighter educational future. Here are some adaptive learning tools that can help your child with ADHD:

- Text-to-speech

- Audio-books

- Word-prediction software

- Speech recognition software

- Talking calculator

- Electronic math worksheet

Techniques for Maintaining Focus and Engagement

Kids with ADHD are usually full of energy and creativity. But keeping them focused can sometimes feel like managing a whirlwind. But do not worry. Here are some techniques to help your child stay on track and conquer learning challenges:

- **Structure and Routine:** To reiterate, predictable routines can help your kids maintain focus. Consistent schedules, clear expectations, and visual aids like checklists and planners can create a sense of order and reduce anxiety.

- **Encourage Breaks:** Think of it as refueling their energy. Breaks aren't distractions; they're essential stops to keep the energy flowing. Picture these breaks as your child's way of getting ready for the next learning adventure. By encouraging breaks, you are ensuring your kid stays alert, engaged, and ready to conquer tasks with a renewed focus.

- **Chunk It Up and Make It Fun:** Overwhelming tasks can be daunting for anyone, especially an ADHD brain. Break down projects into smaller, manageable tasks. Use puzzles, games, and interactive activities to make learning fun and engaging.

- **Positive Reinforcement and Feedback:** Celebrate successes, big and small! Positive reinforcement plays a key role in motivating an ADHD brain. Use specific praise, high-fives, and fun rewards to acknowledge progress and effort.

- **Visual Cues and Clear Instructions:** Remember, clarity is key. Use visual aids like diagrams, charts, and graphic organizers to break down concepts and make them easier to grasp. Give clear and concise instructions, avoiding long-winded explanations that can overwhelm both of you.

- **Sensory Awareness:** Some children with ADHD thrive with sensory input, while others find it distracting. Experiment with fidget tools, calming music, or even aromatherapy to find what works best for your child.

- **Collaboration and Support:** Remember, you are not alone in this. Work with teachers, therapists, and other professionals to create a supportive learning environment. Encourage collaboration and peer support, allowing your child to learn from and motivate others.

The Power of Interactive Learning and Gamification

Traditional learning can feel static and monotonous for children with ADHD. But with interactive learning and gamification, they can engage their attention and unlock their learning potential. Here is why:

- **Increased Engagement:** ADHD brains thrive on novelty and challenge. Interactive learning, with its hands-on activities and immediate feedback, keeps DHD brains engaged and eager for the next step. Gamification adds a layer of fun and competition, turning learning into a thrilling quest.

- **Enhanced Motivation:** Points, badges, and leaderboards tap into the intrinsic reward system of ADHD brains. Every completed task becomes a victory, fueling their desire to keep going and pushing their limits. This positive reinforcement loop builds confidence and encourages persistent effort.

- **Improved Focus:** Gamification helps break down complex tasks into bite-sized challenges, making them less daunting and more manageable. The clear goals and immediate rewards keep the ADHD brain laser-focused on the present moment, minimizing distractions.

- **Development of Executive Function Skills:** Planning, prioritizing, and managing time are crucial skills for everyone, especially children with ADHD. Interactive learning and gamified activities allow children to practice these skills in a safe and engaging environment, building executive function muscles for real-world success.

- **Building Social Connections:** Collaborative games and activities allow children with ADHD to learn from and motivate their peers, promoting a sense of community. This can be especially beneficial for those who often struggle with social interactions.

Here are some strategies to implement interactive learning and gamification:

- Use educational apps and games designed for ADHD learners.

- Incorporate interactive elements into lessons, like quizzes, polls, and group activities.

- Turn real-life tasks into games with point systems and rewards.

- Encourage collaborative learning through games and projects.

Remember, the key is to find what works for your child. Experiment, adapt, and, most importantly, have fun.

Beyond the Classroom

One of the mistakes many parents and caregivers make is that they concentrate more on academic work when dealing with their children with ADHD. To help your kids, you need to look beyond the classroom. You need to look into extracurricular activities that will help your kids. Don't know where to start? Below are some extracurricular activities you can consider.

Sports:

Sports can help children with ADHD to channel that energy into focus and learning. A daily dose of 20 minutes can boost their mental and social skills. But not just any sport will do. Remember, every child with ADHD has a unique superpower set. So, finding the right sport is important. These tips will help you:

- **Choose a sport that sparks your child's interest**: They won't put in the effort necessary to excel if they're not passionate about it. It could be the thrill of team competition, the grace of gymnastics, or the strategic smarts of soccer. Let their enthusiasm be your guide!

- **Look for activities with a low student-to-instructor ratio:** Imagine having a personal trainer for every five kids! That kind of individual attention can work wonders for kids who thrive on focused guidance.

- **Safety First, Fun Always:** Whether it's a group class or one-on-one training, proper supervision is essential. Think of it like having a trustee watching their back and ensuring fair play.

- **Embrace the Outdoors:** While indoor activities like swimming are great, stepping outside adds an extra layer of magic. Fresh air, sunshine, and a dose of nature can work wonders for focus and mood. So, if your child can conquer the pool, imagine their triumph in the open water!

Music:

While sports are often champions for boosting learning for kids with ADHD, don't underestimate the power of music. Unlike sports, which often focus on one side of the brain at a time, music engages both hemispheres simultaneously. Think of it like unlocking a secret level in their brain, granting them the ability to multitask. Learning an instrument or joining a choir becomes a training ground for juggling melodies, rhythms, and even coordination, skills that translate into better focus and attention in all areas of life.

But it doesn't stop there. Music provides access to a vibrant social community. Imagine your child joining a band, orchestra, or choir—a team of fellow music-loving heroes where collaboration and teamwork become second nature. They will build friendships, share triumphs, and learn the crucial skill of synchronizing with others—a valuable lesson both on and off the stage.

So, if you're looking for an activity that unlocks hidden potential, boosts brain power, and fosters social connections, consider the enchanting world of music.

Classic games:

Sometimes, a dusty board game box hides the best playground for learning and growth. Yes, we are talking about the classic, old-fashioned games like chess, checkers, dominoes, and even Bingo. These timeless classics offer a surprising number of benefits:

- **Focus and Attention:** Games like Bingo train your child's focus. Sharp attention is required for tracking numbers, listening for calls, and formulating strategies, a skill that extends to other aspects of life such as schoolwork and chores.

- **Attention Span:** Short and sweet games like checkers and card games are perfect for those with shorter attention spans. Each quick victory becomes a mini-reward, fueling their motivation and encouraging them to tackle longer, more strategic games like chess as their confidence grows.

- **Self-Discipline:** Mastering the art of patience and planning is the key to winning these classic games. Every move requires careful consideration, teaching your child valuable lessons in self-discipline and strategic thinking.

- **Confidence:** Frequent wins in these accessible games build confidence like a stack of building blocks. They learn to celebrate their successes, overcome challenges, and develop a "can-do" attitude that spills over into other aspects of life.

- **Teamwork and Sportsmanship:** Games like chess and checkers aren't just solo adventures. They're opportunities to learn fair play, teamwork, and even gracious defeat. Your child will navigate social interactions, build friendships, and develop valuable communication skills.

Before we move to the next chapter, let me tell you a story about Maya, an eleven-year-old who dislikes school. History, math, and English felt like a puzzle she couldn't solve because of her ADHD. The regular classroom was a bit too cramped for her energy. One day, while exploring the attic in her house, she found old board games, including "History Through Time Travel." Players travel through different times in this game, solving puzzles and facing challenges.

Maya thought, "This isn't boring history; it's an adventure!" She convinced her family to play, and as they journeyed through ancient Egypt and faced Genghis Khan, Maya got hooked. She researched, learned, and drew maps of their time-travel adventures. The game became her secret tool for learning.

Slowly, learning and playing blended. Maya, who struggled with history, now knew the Roman emperors by heart. The battles on the game board turned into victories in class. Her grades improved, and she felt more confident.

Maya's story shows that learning can be exciting. It's not always about textbooks; sometimes, curiosity, imagination, and fun are the best teachers. Maya didn't just get better grades; she found the joy of learning and the magic of discovering things her way. Therefore, if a child appears lost in their studies, perhaps a hidden adventure awaits their discovery.

In conclusion, we explored the various ways kids with ADHD learn best, recognizing that there's no one-size-fits-all approach. Unleashing their potential depends on finding the learning style that resonates with their strengths. Also, customizing learning to match their ADHD profile isn't just about enhancing academic success. It's about shaping positive behaviors, boosting confidence, and sparking a love for learning. Whether it's hands-on activities, musical rhythms, or focused games, each child possesses a learning superpower.

But our journey continues. In the next chapter, we will dive into a crucial ingredient: self-control. This special ability turns knowledge into action, helping kids use their learning styles effectively.

Key Takeaways

- Every child with ADHD possesses a unique learning style, and understanding it is essential for unlocking their potential.

- Tailoring education involves experimenting with diverse learning styles, allowing flexibility to adapt to individual needs.

- Techniques like clear instructions, multi-sensory learning, and adaptive technology enhance focus and engagement for kids with ADHD.

- Interactive learning and gamification not only boost engagement but also develop executive function skills and social connections.

- Extracurricular activities like sports, music, and classic games offer diverse avenues for learning and growth beyond the classroom.

Chapter Three

The Mastery of Impulse-Guiding Self-Control

"Being Spider-Man means control, not just of powers, but of choices. It's about being bigger than the moment."

― ***Spider-Man (Miles Morales).***

Do you know that there is a link between impulsivity and high risks of drinking, smoking, and substance abuse? Adolescents with eating disorders, compulsive gamblers, and suicide attempters all exhibit high levels of impulsivity. Now, that sounds scary, right? Yes, I know. But it is the bitter truth. Impulsive behaviors can be a barricade to a child's long-term success, especially for those with ADHD. But don't you worry; the issue of impulsive behavior is not something that cannot be controlled. And that is why I am dedicating a chapter to address the issue of impulses and self-control to manage them. So, if you are concerned about your child's future, just read on.

But first, what does impulse mean?

Has it ever been done without really thinking about it, like blurting out words, making an unplanned purchase, or crossing the street without checking? That's what we call impulsivity. It's not about being rude or lacking self-discipline; it's just how the brains sometimes work. Kids and teenagers often act on impulse because their brains are still developing, and that's normal. However, when it occurs frequently, it may be associated with specific conditions.

Many people often confuse impulsivity with compulsivity, but these terms have different meanings. Impulsive behaviors are quick, spontaneous actions, like buying something expensive on a whim. Conversely, compulsive behaviors involve repetitive and ritualistic actions, like constantly checking if the stove is off. While impulsivity and compulsivity might seem like opposites, many people have both behaviors.

Even though impulsivity can happen to any individual, people with ADHD are more prone to it because of the uniqueness of their neurological makeup. One key player is the prefrontal cortex (PFC), which is in charge of controlling impulses. People with ADHD often have issues in this area, affecting their ability to stop and think before acting. Another factor is the brain's reward system, where dopamine plays a big role. In ADHD, this system can be a bit off, impacting motivation and self-control. Norepinephrine, which is associated with attention and focus, also plays a role.

Think of the brain like a network—the CSTC circuit. It involves different regions coordinating to control movement and attention. In ADHD, this network might not work as smoothly, leading to difficulties in managing impulses. Beyond these, other brain messengers like serotonin and glutamate add to the mix, affecting mood and attention.

Recognizing triggers and patterns of impulsive behavior

While we all experience flashes of impulsivity from time to time, frequent impulsive behavior can sometimes indicate an underlying condition like ADHD, bipolar disorder, or obsessive-compulsive disorder (OCD). Aside from that, different factors might contribute to the development of impulsivity. Some of those factors include:

- **Genetics:** There is a genetic component to some of the disorders associated with impulsivity, such as ADHD and bipolar disorder. Having a family history of these conditions might increase the risk.

- **Environment:** Early childhood experiences such as trauma, neglect, or abuse can impact brain development and increase the risk of impulsive behavior later in life. Chronic stress and exposure to violence can also play a role.

- **Brain Function:** Dysfunction in certain brain regions responsible for planning, decision-making, and impulse control can contribute to impulsive behavior. Neurological conditions like epilepsy or brain injuries can also be factors.

- **Physical Changes in the Brain:** Age-related changes in brain chemistry, particularly dopamine levels, can contribute to increased impulsivity in older adults. Additionally, conditions like Alzheimer's disease can also affect impulse control.

- **Substance Abuse Disorders:** Drugs and alcohol can impair judgment and decrease inhibition, increasing the likelihood of impulsive behaviors.

Now, let's go to the patterns.

Impulsivity can manifest in diverse ways, and its expression varies depending on the underlying factors. There are different patterns in which impulsivity can be expressed in children. Some of the examples are:

- **Having frequent outbursts:**

Frequent and random outbursts, from bursts of anger to uncontrollable laughter, can leave peers feeling confused and unsafe. For instance, a child suddenly throws a mini tantrum in the middle of a game, leaving everyone around them startled and hesitant to re-engage.

- **Throwing tantrums:**

Explosive tantrums, complete with yelling, crying, and even throwing objects, can be especially damaging to relationships. Imagine a child's frustration at a lost game erupting into a full-blown meltdown, causing friends to scatter and avoid future interactions.

- **Interrupting friends in class:**

Constant interruptions in class and during play can disrupt the flow of conversation and activities, making it difficult for others to focus or enjoy themselves. Children with impulsive behavior can blurt out answers before questions are finished, frustrating classmates eager to participate properly.

- **Non-stop talking:**

Imagine a child who dominates conversations, bombarding everyone with a constant stream of words, often interrupting others or ignoring social cues. This incessant talking can be overwhelming and leave others feeling unheard and frustrated. While some children are naturally talkative, the key difference lies in their ability to read social cues and adjust their communication accordingly. For a child with impulsive behavior, the urge to talk can overpower any sense of timing or respect for others' space.

- **Being restless or excessively active:**

This child with impulsive behavior will always want to be in motion, constantly squirming, tapping their feet, or bouncing around. This restlessness can also be a sign of pent-up energy or difficulty regulating their physical responses to internal stimuli. Yes, some children are naturally energetic; they should be able to focus and maintain stillness when necessary. A child with impulsive behavior will find it difficult to sit still and engage in focused activities.

- **Easily getting frustrated:**

Children with impulsive behavior usually get easily frustrated and give up quickly. For instance, they can throw down their paintbrush after a minor mistake, discouraging other children who are trying to learn from their challenges.

- **Impatience:**

For this child, waiting feels like an eternity. They tap their feet, ask, "Are we there yet?" every minute, and may even melt down if their desires aren't met instantly. This can lead to disruptive behavior in any setting where waiting is inevitable, from restaurants to playdates.

- **Inability to handle humor:**

Some children with impulsive behavior can't take a joke. Even mild teasing, playful humor, or friendly jabs can trigger tears, anger, or even physical reactions. This makes it difficult for them to participate in playful banter, navigate social interactions, and learn from gentle teasing, a common childhood experience.

- **Inability to handle criticism:**

Some children crumble at the slightest criticism. They cry, defend, or even withdraw due to feedback, whether in school or at home. This can hinder their learning, self-esteem, and ability to accept constructive feedback, a vital part of personal growth.

> *"In times of crisis, the wise build bridges while the foolish build barriers."* - **Black Panther**

Strategies for Self-Regulation

It is not only necessary to know about impulsiveness and its expressions, but it is also important to know how to practice self-regulation. In this section, you will learn how to use the strategies of self-regulation, especially for kids. These tips will help you to help your child manage their impulsivity. Let's proceed.

● Teach them to name their feeling:

Help your little ones express their feelings by teaching them to put words to their emotions. Picture a scenario: a child who doesn't understand how to say, "I'm angry," might resort to hitting when upset. Another child, unable to vocalize, "I feel sad," may end up dramatically throwing themselves on the floor and letting out a scream.

So, start with the basics. Show them the emotional ABCs: angry, sad, excited, surprised, worried, and scared. Help them understand that feelings are okay, but actions matter too. Make it clear that while it's perfectly fine to feel angry, it's not okay to express it by hitting, kicking, or yelling. This lesson isn't just about labeling emotions; it's also about distinguishing between feelings and behaviors.

Once they grasp this, they'll be better at telling you how they feel instead of acting it out. When they can articulate their emotions in words, they're more likely to feel understood and supported, reducing the urge to resort to impulsive actions.

- **Let them repeat directions:**

Make sure your child isn't jumping into action without catching the directions first. Especially for kids with ADHD, not paying attention can lead to impulsive behavior. Therefore, it's crucial to keep them focused and attentive. You wouldn't want them sprinting off before they even know what's going on, right?

Here's a trick: Teach them to listen closely by having them repeat your instructions before doing anything. Before you start laying out the game plan, say, "Before you move, tell me what I just said." After you've spilled the details, throw in a quick quiz: "Alright, what did I just ask you to do?"

Only when they can smoothly replay your instructions—whether it's cleaning their room or stashing away homework—should they dive into action. And let's keep it simple; instructions should be easy to follow with as few steps as possible.

- **Teach them problem-solving:**

Show your child that, when it comes to problems, there's more than one way to crack the code. Whether fixing a wonky bicycle chain or tackling a tricky math problem, they have options.

Encourage them to put on their thinking caps and brainstorm at least five ways to solve the problem. Once they have their list, help them figure out which solution is the smartest move. With some practice, they will get the hang of thinking before they make a move.

- **Teach them anger management:**

Sometimes, low frustration tolerance can kick impulsive outbursts into high gear. So, it's important to teach your child some anger management skills to handle their emotions.

Teach them some anger management skills, like taking a few deep breaths or lapping around the house to burn off that steam. The key here is to show them how to hit pause, make smarter choices, or find their calm-down spot before acting impulsively.

- **Alter their response:**

Help children discover alternative responses instead of reacting impulsively. For instance, suggest that they cross their arms or hug themselves when angry. For school-aged children, teach them phrases like "So what?" or "Was that funny?" to handle bullying or teasing without letting it deeply affect them. Another effective strategy is teaching your child to divert their attention by engaging in activities like counting tiles, counting numbers backward, drawing, playing a musical instrument, or painting. This empowers them to respond thoughtfully and maintain better self-regulation.

- **Be a model:**

Serve as a positive example for your child by being mindful of your actions, words, and behavior. Share your own experiences, including mistakes, and showcase how you exercise self-control. For instance, express, "I need some time to cool off because I am angry," and take a moment alone in your room. Your child will observe these positive behaviors and likely emulate them when facing challenges. Additionally, instill the value of respecting others in your child, creating a foundation for positive behavior in various situations.

- **Establish a reward system:**

Kids learn best by doing, so what better way to teach delayed gratification than by making it fun? You can introduce a token system where good choices and completed tasks earn "coins" of appreciation. These can be actual tokens, stickers, or even virtual points on a chart.

Have various forms of rewards. Some quick wins, like extra story time, cost just a few tokens, while larger adventures, like a trip to the zoo, might require saving up a treasure trove. This teaches kids the joys of delayed gratification—the bigger the prize, the sweeter the wait.

As your child collects tokens, celebrate their progress. Talk about the excitement of saving up and the feeling of accomplishment when they finally reach their goal. This positive reinforcement strengthens their self-control muscles, helping them resist impulsive choices and master the art of waiting.

Remember, the key is to make it a positive experience. Keep the rewards enticing, track progress visually, and, most importantly, shower them with praise when they reach their milestones.

The Role of Mindfulness and Meditation

Mindfulness and meditation can play a powerful role in managing impulsivity by attacking it from multiple angles:

- **Increased Self-Awareness:**

Mindfulness practices train your child to pay attention to their thoughts, emotions, and bodily sensations without judgment. This increased awareness allows them to recognize the early warning signs of impulsivity, like rising anxiety or cravings, before they lead to an impulsive action. Also, meditation helps them observe their thoughts and emotions without getting swept away by them. This creates a space between the urge and the action, giving them time to choose a conscious response instead of a knee-jerk reaction.

- **Improved Emotional Regulation:**

Mindfulness practices teach your child to manage difficult emotions like anger, frustration, or boredom, which can often trigger impulsive behavior. By learning to notice and accept these emotions without reacting, they can lessen their grip and make more deliberate choices. Meditation teaches the brain to focus on the present moment, reducing rumination on past events or worrying about the future, both of which can contribute to impulsivity.

- **Enhanced Impulse Control:**

Mindfulness practices help children develop cognitive flexibility and the ability to shift their attention and thoughts away from tempting situations or intrusive urges. This allows them to consider alternative responses and choose the most appropriate one, even if it's not the most impulsive.

Meditation strengthens the prefrontal cortex, the brain region responsible for planning, decision-making, and impulse control. Regular practice can increase its activity, leading to better control over impulsive urges.

- **Increased Stress Resilience:**

Mindfulness practices teach children to manage stress effectively, which is a major trigger for impulsive behavior. By learning to relax and respond calmly to stressful situations, they can reduce the likelihood of acting impulsively.

Meditation cultivates inner peace and calmness, even in challenging situations. This increased emotional resilience makes them less likely to react impulsively to external stressors.

Ultimately, mindfulness and meditation don't offer a quick fix for impulsivity, but their cumulative benefits can significantly improve their ability to manage impulsive urges and make more conscious choices.

Below are some mindfulness meditation games for the whole family, especially one with a child with ADHD. Try incorporating these activities into your routine:

   a. **Breathing Practice:**

Gather your favorite stuffed animals for each participant. Lie on the floor together, placing a stuffed animal on each person's stomach. Instruct everyone to take deep, slow breaths, observing the movement of the stuffed animal. Discuss what each person notices. This activity promotes self-soothing and helps calm hyperactive behaviors.

   b. **Sitting Meditation:**

Select a quiet time, such as before a meal or bedtime, and introduce the idea of playing a relaxing game. Arrange two chairs, or use the child's bed. Ask your child to sit with feet flat on the floor, back straight, and hands on their knees. Using a gentle, slow voice, guide them to focus on a spot on the wall. Instruct them to breathe in slowly, hold it, and exhale slowly.

If they feel restless, encourage them to acknowledge it silently and remain still. Emphasize the idea of being like a statue, solely focusing on their breath. Start with one to two minutes and gradually extend the duration, ensuring it aligns with your child's age.

c. **Walking Meditation:**

Adapted from Buddhist practices, walking meditation encourages mindfulness during movement. Whether indoors or outdoors, introduce a walking game to your child. Walk together at a very slow pace, focusing on each step. Offer gentle instructions such as, "Take a slow step forward, feel the bend in your knee, and notice how your foot touches the floor.

When you feel the urge to speed up or walk in a crooked line, silently say, 'I am tired of walking slow and straight, but I'll keep doing it.' Breathe slowly and pay attention to how your body feels when moving slowly after a fast-paced day." Talk about implementing this skill at school to promote slow and mindful walking in the hallways.

d. **Freeze Game**:

In this lively game, play music and let your child dance or be silly in the room. After a few minutes, call out "freeze!" Encourage your child to stop and remain perfectly still. During this stillness, guide them with the affirmation, "Notice how your body feels standing still compared to when it was dancing. Stay very still, acknowledging if any part of your body wants to move or feels tired. Instead of moving, take deep breaths and tell yourself, 'It's okay to be tired or want to wiggle, but for now, stay nice and still.'" The freezing period lasts about a minute before the music resumes, and the freezing duration increases with each round.

Setting Up a Home Environment That Encourages Self-Control

In helping your child to develop self-control, the environment of the home determines the effectiveness of your strategies. The following are tips that help you have a suitable home environment that encourages self–control:

- **Ensure clear and consistent communication:**

Express expectations plainly and frequently, emphasizing the behaviors that matter. Simple phrases like "Reading time is quiet time" or "Take turns with favorite toys" lay the foundation for understanding. Regularly reinforce rules and expectations, creating an environment where children are reminded when it's time to follow them.

- **Establish a routine:**

Establish routines that provide structure. Even though young children might not grasp the concept of time, they thrive on predictability. A regular schedule, such as moving from story time to outdoor play, helps them anticipate transitions. This predictability can be especially helpful for active children, increasing their capacity to engage in quieter activities.

- **Incorporate Happy Movement:**

Infuse moments of joyous movement throughout the day. Recognize that young children have limited attention spans, and to cater to this, alternate learning activities that require focused attention with opportunities for independent play and activities involving physical movement. By balancing quiet, focused moments with energetic, movement-based ones, children can better regulate their energy levels and attention.

- **Gamify Learning:**

Transforming learning into a game can be a powerful tool. Computer and concentration-style card games enhance working memory in young children. Active games like "Red Light, Green Light" and "Freeze," where children dance to music and stop when it halts, require the exertion of self-control. Even during music time, incorporating activities like playing rhythm instruments in sync with a beat fosters self-regulation. Introducing various games and activities allows children to take charge of their bodies, voices, and minds while thinking they're simply having fun.

- **Promote Pro-social Behaviors:**

Encourage the development of self-control by fostering pro-social behaviors—actions that consider others' feelings and welfare. This not only creates positive interactions with peers but also correlates with academic and social-emotional skills. You can guide children by setting clear expectations for sharing and helping others, modeling these actions themselves, and providing individual, positive attention to each child. Reinforce the idea that helping others not only benefits them, but also brings happiness to everyone involved.

In conclusion, while a playful outburst or impatient demand may seem like passing moments in childhood, the ripple effect of impulsivity can extend far beyond the immediate incident. Unchecked impulsive behaviors can hinder a child's long-term success. This is where the crucial role of self-control comes in. Teaching children to pause, reflect, and choose their responses empowers them to break this damaging chain.

The next chapter dives deeper into the unique social landscape children with ADHD navigate. Recognizing their specific challenges is key to providing appropriate support and guidance.

Key Takeaways

- Impulsive behaviors, such as blurting out words, are common in children due to the development of their brains.

- People with ADHD are more prone to impulsivity due to differences in the prefrontal cortex and neurotransmitters like dopamine and norepinephrine.

- Impulsivity can manifest in various ways in children, including frequent outbursts, tantrums, interrupting others, non-stop talking, restlessness, frustration, impatience, inability to handle humor, and difficulty handling criticism.

- Factors contributing to impulsivity include genetics, environment, brain function, physical changes in the brain, and substance abuse disorders.

- **Strategies for self-regulation in children include:**
  - ❖ Teaching them to name their feelings
  - ❖ Having them repeat directions before acting
  - ❖ Teaching problem-solving and anger management
  - ❖ Altering their response to triggers
  - ❖ Being a positive role model, and establishing a reward system.

Chapter Four

The Social Maze - Navigating Friendships with and without ADHD

"In times of crisis, the wise build bridges while the foolish build barriers."

- Black Panther (T' Challa)

Have you ever wondered how kids learn to relate to one another? You know, many times, kids just pick up certain behaviors when interacting with other people.

The question is: how do they learn it? The truth is that the early years are a time of incredible learning for children. From those wobbly first steps to turning babbles into words, they soak up everything around them. Amidst all the toys and finger painting, something crucial is happening: social interaction.

So, what exactly is social interaction?

Think of social interaction as a venue for development. Every shared laugh, every little disagreement over a toy, and every attempt at a handshake is a chance for your child to learn and grow. They're figuring out how to handle feelings, read body language, and see things from different points of view.

Unlike adults, kids learn best by doing things themselves. Watching others play is okay, but it's the active playing, sharing, and taking turns that teach them. They learn how to make deals, enjoy working together, and why it's important to respect personal space—skills that will help them in all sorts of social situations, from school to work.

The good things that come from early social interaction go way beyond the playground. A child who learns to connect with others is more likely to feel good about themselves, handle tough times better, and deal with problems calmly. These are the building blocks for future success, setting the stage for strong relationships in personal and professional life.

But for kids with ADHD, social interaction can be a bit challenging. But don't worry, there are always ways to help your kids develop social skills that will help their social interaction. But before we delve into addressing the issue, let's talk about the impact of ADHD on social skills. That way, you have adequate knowledge about what we are dealing with.

- **Difficulty Picking up on Social Cues:**

Children with ADHD often encounter challenges in picking up on social cues. This difficulty can stem from a tendency to become easily distracted or hyper-focused on their thoughts and activities. As a result, they may not fully register the subtleties of nonverbal communication, such as facial expressions, body language, or tone of voice.

They might struggle to understand when it's their turn to speak, when someone is expressing discomfort, or when a conversation is taking a subtle turn. This difficulty in reading social cues may lead to unintentional interruptions, as they may not grasp the appropriate timing to contribute to a conversation. Additionally, they might inadvertently break social rules or norms, not out of defiance but due to a genuine oversight in recognizing these cues.

- **Challenges in maintaining friendships:**

Children with ADHD often face difficulties sustaining friendships, and this struggle is rooted in several aspects of their behavior and social interactions. One significant factor contributing to challenges in maintaining friendships is the tendency to exhibit intensity and demands in their interactions. Due to the nature of their condition, they may become engrossed in specific topics or activities, sometimes to an extent that may overwhelm their peers. This intensity can create an imbalance in the relationship, as others may find it challenging to match the fervor or may feel pressured by their level of engagement.

Also, taking turns and sharing are fundamental social skills that are critical for the development and maintenance of friendships. However, children with ADHD may find these aspects challenging due to impulsivity and difficulty with self-regulation.

They may unintentionally dominate conversations, activities, or resources without being aware of the impact on their friends. This can create an environment where peers feel overlooked or overshadowed, leading to strained relationships.

- **Going off-topic:**

Children with ADHD may find it a bit tricky to stay on track during discussions. Their minds, often filled with a constant stream of thoughts, can lead to unintentional diversions from the main topic.

This off-topic drift is linked to the unique workings of their brain. The challenges of filtering out irrelevant thoughts and the constant influx of ideas can create a mental environment where maintaining a clear focus on a conversation becomes a bit more demanding. It's akin to juggling multiple thoughts simultaneously, making it easier for the primary topic to slip away momentarily.

Amid these cognitive challenges, they may misinterpret what others are saying. The interplay between attention and distraction may result in missing subtle cues or nuances in communication. As a consequence, their interpretations might differ from the intended message.

- **Meltdowns:**

For kids with ADHD, emotions can sometimes feel like a rollercoaster ride. When upset, they might struggle to keep their reactions in check and may end up lashing out. The intensity of their emotional responses can make it challenging for them to express themselves calmly. In some situations, children with ADHD may experience meltdowns, even at an age where such reactions are typically less common. These meltdowns can be disproportionate to the situation at hand.

Social Expectations and Misunderstandings

For many kids with ADHD, moving through daily life can feel like figuring out a puzzle with hidden rules. How they process and show themselves might be a bit different, leading to misunderstandings. Let's break down a few common misconceptions about ADHD behaviors and see how they can affect things.

- **Fidgeting:**

When you see a kid tapping a pen or wiggling in a chair, it might look like they're being disrespectful. But actually, it's their way of staying focused. Fidgeting helps their minds stay on track. Instead of thinking of it as a problem, understanding this can help everyone accept it and find ways to work with it.

- **Hyperactivity:**

Sometimes, a kid with ADHD might seem like they have too much energy—running around, bouncing off walls. It's not about being disobedient; it's just how ADHD shows itself. By giving them structured ways to use that energy and being patient, we can turn what might seem like naughty behavior into a wellspring of creativity and excitement.

- **Daydreaming:**

When a kid with ADHD seems to be daydreaming, it might look like they're not interested. But actually, it's their active minds exploring different ideas. Daydreaming for them isn't a lack of interest; it's a way to find creative solutions. Acknowledging this and creating moments for structured daydreaming can reveal the incredible potential hidden in those seemingly absent moments.

These misunderstandings don't just stop at the surface; they create a ripple effect that reaches deep into the lives of children with ADHD. Here are some lasting effects:

- **Negative Judgments:** Children with ADHD might be unfairly seen as rude, disobedient, or lazy due to these misinterpretations. Internalizing these negative labels can significantly affect their self-esteem and confidence.

- **Disciplinary Measures:** Punishing behaviors like fidgeting, hyperactivity, or daydreaming as if they were intentional actions can make things worse. It exacerbates the existing challenges and creates a feeling of injustice, making it harder for children with ADHD to navigate their surroundings.

- **Social Exclusion:** Misunderstandings can lead to social isolation, with peers not fully understanding and, at times, excluding children with ADHD. This struggle to build friendships and form healthy social connections can have a lasting impact on their social well-being.

Friendships with Peers with ADHD

Kids with ADHD often find themselves in a social world that's a bit different. Their active minds, impulsive actions, and attention struggles can make creating and keeping friendships a bit tricky. But what if the secret to their social triumphs is right within their community? Building friendships with other kids who also have ADHD can be a game-changer, offering a special support network and opening up a world of understanding and acceptance.

Here's how connecting within the ADHD community can make a difference:

- **Shared Experiences:** Kids with ADHD understand each other's challenges because they share similar experiences. This similar experience helps them to bond with each other.

- **Unique Support System:** The ADHD community becomes a built-in support system. Friends who "get it" can offer encouragement during tough times and celebrate successes in a way that others might not fully understand.

- **Embracing Differences**: Within the ADHD community, differences are celebrated rather than judged. Kids can be themselves without feeling the need to fit into traditional molds, fostering an environment of acceptance.

- **Learning Together:** Friends with ADHD can navigate strategies and coping mechanisms together. Learning from each other's experiences becomes a shared journey toward growth and self-discovery.

- **Boosting Confidence:** Being part of a community where ADHD is not a barrier but a shared trait can boost confidence. Kids learn that they are not alone and that their uniqueness is something to be proud of.

Creating opportunities for these friendships to blossom can be as simple as:

- **Encouraging peer interaction:** Organize play dates, group activities, or ADHD-friendly social groups.

- **Open communication:** Talk to your child about ADHD and its impact on friendships. Encourage them to be open and understanding with others who share similar challenges.

- **Focus on shared interests:** Look for activities that both children enjoy, whether it's sports, art, music, or building things. Shared passions can be the bridge to strong friendships.

Conflict Resolution among Children with ADHD

Navigating conflict can be tricky for anyone, but for children with ADHD, emotions, and impulsivity can add an extra layer of complexity. However, promoting healthy conflict resolution skills is crucial for their social and emotional development.

Now, let's equip them with some conflict-resolution tools:

- Teach them to recognize their triggers and emotional cues. Suggest taking deep breaths or stepping away from the situation to calm down before engaging in the conflict.

- Please encourage them to truly listen to the other person's perspective without interrupting. They can do this by mirroring what they hear or asking clarifying questions.

- Teach them to use "I" statements, not "you" attacks. Shifting the focus to how they feel ("I feel hurt when you...") instead of blaming the other person ("You always...")

Remember, conflict resolution is a skill that needs practice and support. Here are some ways to help:

- **Role-Playing:** Practice different conflict scenarios in a safe environment. This allows them to experiment with different approaches and build confidence.

- **Positive Reinforcement:** Celebrate their successes in resolving conflicts calmly and constructively. This reinforces positive behavior and encourages them to keep trying.

- **Open Communication:** Create a safe space where they can openly talk about their challenges and frustrations with conflict.

Building Bridges with Non-ADHD Peers

For children with ADHD, the social landscape can be challenging because of their unique neurodiversity. Connecting with non-ADHD peers can be both exciting and challenging. But fear not. There are many ways to help your child connect with their ADHD peers. But first, let's acknowledge the differences that might lead to misunderstandings:

- **Energy Levels:** Children with ADHD often operate at a higher RPM, bouncing with ideas and needing frequent movement. Non-ADHD peers might prefer a calmer and faster interaction.

- **Communication Styles:** ADHD brains can ping-pong between topics, while non-ADHD peers might rely on linear conversations.

- **Focus and Attention:** Children with ADHD may struggle to focus for extended periods, whereas non-ADHD peers might find distractions disruptive.

Now that you understand the challenges, here are ways to foster a connection between your child and non-ADHD peers. Although I have explained some of these points earlier, they're worth mentioning again because they are crucial in helping your child's relationship.

- Encourage open conversations about ADHD with your child and their peers. Sharing accurate information about the condition promotes empathy and understanding.

- Highlight the unique strengths and talents that children with ADHD bring to the table. Their creativity, enthusiasm, and out-of-the-box thinking can enrich friendships and group activities.

- Find common interests and activities that allow children with and without ADHD to connect and bond.

- Encourage active listening and perspective-taking. Role-playing scenarios can help children understand how others might perceive their actions and words.

Social skills exercise: Let's Chat Together

We designed this activity to help your child with ADHD understand that conversations are a shared experience where everyone gets a chance to speak and listen. It's all about ditching interruptions and embracing the art of dialogue. Let's guide your child through the essentials of sparking and extending a conversation.

Getting the Conversation Rolling: Help your child initiate discussions using friendly prompts like:

- How's your day going?

- Do you have a favorite (teacher, activity, video game)?

- What was (an event) like?

- Hey, I noticed...

Taking Conversations to New Heights: Encourage your child to keep the conversation ball rolling with these tips:

- Ask questions to dive deeper into the other person's world.

- Discover shared interests and experiences.

- Comment on what's been said and throw in a question for good measure.

Mastering the Art of Exchange: Explore different phases of a conversation like a well-rehearsed play:

- Greeting: Kick things off with a warm "Hello" or a casual "How's it going?"

- Choosing a Topic: Dive into shared interests like recent vacations, sports, or school experiences.

Expanding on Topics: Encourage your child to build on the discussion:

- Speaker 1: "This summer, I want to camp more."
- Speaker 2: "Me too! Where do you usually go?"

Extra Strategies to Enhance Social Skills

Decode Signals: Teach your child to read both verbal and non-verbal cues, like body language, to understand how the other person feels.

- **Active Listening:** Emphasize the importance of not just hearing but actively absorbing information. Looking engaged is key.

- **Supportive Comments:** Show your child the power of affirming comments. A simple "Oh, wow" or "That sounds tough" lets the speaker know they're being heard.

- **Gesture Game:** Instruct your child to nod and lean forward to express genuine interest in the conversation.

By turning conversations into a shared adventure, your child can navigate social interactions with newfound confidence and finesse.

Social interactions are vital for a child's development. For children with ADHD, navigating unique challenges in understanding cues, maintaining friendships, and mastering conversation requires specific strategies. Embracing the ADHD community, fostering connections with peers, and honing conflict resolution skills are important. With understanding, support, and tailored approaches, children with ADHD can build meaningful connections and strong relationships.

The journey to social interaction doesn't end here. In the next one, we will explore emotional intelligence, a key factor in having effective social interaction.

Key Takeaways

- Childhood lays the foundation for lifelong social skills, and active engagement shapes emotional intelligence.

- Children with ADHD face unique social hurdles, from reading cues to maintaining friendships, requiring tailored support.

- Misinterpretations of ADHD behaviors can lead to negative judgments, disciplinary measures, and social exclusion, impacting self-esteem.

- Fostering friendships within the ADHD community provides a supportive network, celebrating shared experiences and differences.

- Equipping children with ADHD with conflict resolution tools involves recognizing triggers, active listening, and using "I" statements.

- Connecting with non-ADHD peers requires open conversations, highlighting strengths, and finding common ground amidst differing energy levels and communication styles.

Chapter Five

Emotional Superheroes - Harnessing Emotional Intelligence

"It's not about what you deserve; it's about what you believe. And I believe in love."

-Wonder Woman

Ever wonder why some kids seem good at handling their feelings and making friends easily. It's often because they have strong emotional intelligence. Emotional intelligence (EQ) means being able to understand and control your own emotions as well as other people's emotions. Emotional intelligence is important for everyone, but for kids with ADHD, it can be a superpower.

Why is EQ so important for kids with ADHD?

Kids with ADHD often experience intense emotions, and they may struggle to manage them effectively. This can lead to meltdowns, outbursts, and difficulty with relationships. High EQ can help them:

- **Understand their emotions:** When a child with ADHD can identify their feelings, they can start to understand why they're behaving in certain ways. This can assist them in taking charge of their behavior, rather than letting their emotions dictate it.

- **Cope with frustration and anger:** ADHD can make it hard to stay calm when things don't go your way. However, with strong emotional regulation skills, kids can learn to express their frustration in healthy ways and avoid meltdowns.

- **Build and maintain friendships:** Understanding and responding to the emotions of others is key to building strong relationships. Kids with ADHD who have high EQ are more likely to have successful friendships and feel supported by their peers.

- **Improve academic performance:** EQ can improve academic performance in children with ADHD. This is likely because kids with strong EQ are better able to focus, manage their time, and cope with stress.

Now that you know why emotional intelligence is vital for your kids, let's explore some components of emotional intelligence.

- **Self-awareness:**

Self-awareness is when we recognize and understand our feelings. It's not just about knowing what we feel but also understanding how our actions and emotions affect others. To be self-aware, we need to correctly identify our emotions, monitor them, and see how they connect to our behavior.

When we're self-aware, we know our strengths and weaknesses, stay open to new things, and learn from our interactions. People with self-awareness usually have a good sense of humor, confidence in themselves, and awareness of how others see them.

- **Self-regulation**

Self-regulation, as part of our emotional intelligence, goes beyond just recognizing emotions. It's about managing and controlling our emotions without locking them away. Instead of suppressing feelings, we express them at the right time and place. Self-regulation involves expressing emotions appropriately.

Those who excel in self-regulation are adaptable to change, skilled at handling conflict, and adept at diffusing tense situations. Strong self-regulators are often conscientious, considerate of their influence on others, and take responsibility for their actions.

- **Social skills:**

Understanding emotions goes beyond just knowing our own and others. It's about applying this knowledge in our daily interactions. Interacting effectively is a key emotional intelligence skill involving active listening, good verbal and nonverbal communication, and persuasiveness. These skills help build meaningful relationships and deepen our understanding of others and ourselves.

- **Empathy:**

Empathy, a vital emotional intelligence skill, means understanding others' feelings and seeing things from their perspective. It involves recognizing someone's emotional state and understanding the reasons behind it.

Empathy guides our interactions with various people, allowing us to understand power dynamics in relationships and comprehend how they affect emotions and behaviors. This understanding helps interpret situations influenced by power dynamics more effectively.

- **Motivation:**

Emotionally intelligent individuals find motivation beyond external rewards like fame or money. Inner needs and goals drive them, as they seek intrinsic rewards. This type of motivation propels them into a state of flow, where they fully engage in an activity and strive for exceptional experiences.

Motivated individuals with emotional intelligence are action-oriented, set goals, have a strong need for achievement, and continuously seek improvement. They are committed, take initiative, and thrive on pushing themselves to do better.

Understanding and Managing One's Emotions

An important aspect of emotional intelligence is teaching your child how to understand and manage their emotions. This section will cover that. First, let's start with how your child can learn to understand their emotions.

- **Teach them to create space:**

Emotions don't come with warnings; they just happen. As parents, you can empower your child with a valuable skill: creating space. When anger or frustration hits, encourage them to take a breath to slow down that instant between what triggers their emotions and how they respond.

- **Encourage them to note their feeling:**

Encouraging your child to notice and understand their emotions is a valuable skill for navigating the complexities of their feelings. Guide your child to tune into themselves; ask, where do they feel sensations in their body? Is their stomach uneasy? Is their heart racing? Do they sense tension in their neck or head? Connecting physical symptoms to emotions provides vital clues.

- **Teach them to name their emotions:**

Once your child has tuned into their emotions, the next empowering step is to give a name to what they're feeling. Encourage them to ask: Is it anger, sadness, disappointment, or maybe resentment? Emphasize that it's okay to experience a mix of emotions simultaneously. Dive deeper into the layers—if it's fear, what exactly are they afraid of? If anger is present, what triggers it?

- **Encourage them to accept their emotions:**

Teach your child the importance of accepting their emotions as a natural and valid part of being human. Instead of self-criticism for feeling angry or scared, encourage self-compassion. Emphasize that everyone experiences a range of emotions, and there's no need to judge or blame oneself for these feelings.

- **Teach them mindfulness:**

Introduce your child to the practice of mindfulness, a powerful tool for staying grounded in the present moment. Encourage them to engage their senses, observing their surroundings without judgment.

Now that your kid can recognize their emotions, let's proceed to teach them the strategies they need to manage their emotions.

- **Teach them to identify triggers:**

Help your child understand and manage their emotions by identifying and exploring triggers. While it's natural to feel a range of emotions, recognizing patterns or situations that intensify these feelings is key. Encourage curiosity and honesty. Ask questions like, "What happened that made you feel this way?"

By identifying triggers, your child gains insight into the root causes of emotional reactions. For instance, you can trace a child's upset when sharing toys back to a specific experience. Understanding these triggers empowers your child to reduce their impact and navigate emotions with greater ease.

- **Encourage them to listen to body signals:**

Guide your child to tune into their physical sensations as a valuable tool in managing emotions. Encourage them to notice if they feel hungry or tired, as these factors can influence emotional intensity. By understanding the connection between physical well-being and emotions, your child gains insight into their body's signals. If they identify hunger or tiredness, addressing these underlying issues can positively impact their emotional responses. It's a simple yet powerful way for your child to take charge of their emotional well-being.

- **Teach them that narrative matters:**

Teach your child to reflect on the stories they tell themselves about situations. Explain that in the absence of information, our minds tend to fill in gaps with our interpretations. Encourage them to question their assumptions and explore alternative explanations. For instance, if a friend doesn't reply, rather than assuming they don't care, help your child consider other possibilities like busyness or forgetfulness. Teaching them to approach situations with openness can lead to more balanced emotional responses.

- **Teach them the power of positive self-talk:**

Teach your child the power of positive self-talk during intense emotions. Explain that when feelings become overwhelming, negative self-talk might take over. Encourage them to treat themselves with empathy and replace negativity with positive affirmations. For instance, instead of saying, *"I messed up again,"* guide them to say, *"I always try my best."* This shift in self-talk can help them navigate emotions more constructively, allowing room for self-compassion.

- **Let them know they have a choice:**

Teach your child the empowering skill of choosing their responses to emotions. Help them understand that, in many situations, they have a choice in how they react. If, for instance, they often respond to anger with harsh words, discuss the negative impact it can have on relationships. Encourage them to recognize the power of choosing a different response, such as expressing their feelings calmly instead of lashing out.

Recognizing the Emotions of Others

After teaching your kids how to understand and manage their emotions, it is important to teach them to identify other people's emotions. This way, you are helping them develop a strong emotional intelligence. Below are strategies to employ:

- **Facial expressions:** Use flashcards or mirrors to practice identifying basic emotions like happiness, sadness, anger, and fear through facial expressions. Play games like "Guess the Feeling," where you act out different emotions and have your child guess what you're feeling.

- **Body language:** Pay attention to posture, gestures, and eye contact as clues to emotions. Create stories or act out scenarios where characters express different emotions through their body language.

- **Visual aids:** Utilize charts, pictures, or even emojis to associate specific emotions with their corresponding facial expressions, body language, and even sounds.

- **Active listening:** Train your child to pay attention not just to the words but also to the tone of voice, volume, and pace of speech. Play recordings of different voices expressing emotions and ask them to identify the feelings based on the audio cues.

- **Environmental clues:** Discuss how the environment can reflect emotions. For example, a messy room might suggest frustration, while a quiet space might indicate sadness. Encourage your child to observe their surroundings and make inferences about the emotions at play.

- **Role-playing:** Act out different scenarios were characters experience various emotions. Ask your child to identify the emotions and suggest appropriate responses.

- **Vocabulary building:** Introduce and practice a wide range of words related to emotions, from basic terms like *"happy"* and *"sad"* to more nuanced expressions like "frustrated," "disappointed," or "excited."

- **Emotional journaling:** Encourage your child to keep a journal where they write about their own emotions and those they observe in others. This helps them reflect on their experiences and develop emotional awareness.

- **Storytelling and games:** Read stories with strong emotional themes and discuss the characters' feelings. Play games like "Would You Rather" or "Finish the Story" to prompt discussions about emotions and decision-making based on emotional cues.

Techniques for Dealing with Anger, Frustration, and Anxiety

A child with ADHD is prone to be angry, frustrated, and anxious. The following techniques can help you address the challenges.

- **Reduce screen time:**

Prolonged electronic use not only dulls the mind but also hinders physical activity and in-person social engagements. While some screen time can be beneficial, we should minimize exceeding two hours per day. Encouraging alternative activities and face-to-face interactions can contribute to a more fulfilling and less anxiety-inducing lifestyle.

- **Teach your kid that anger is not an outcome but a signal:**

Teach them to pause when angry, asking, *"Why am I angry?"* Articulating the cause can enhance emotional control. Additionally, if anger stems from mistreatment or danger, teach them to seek help confidently.

- **Keep a journal:**

Maintain a daily journal to track your child's behaviors. Consistently documenting their actions allows you to identify patterns over time. After a month, reviewing these entries may unveil valuable insights, offering clues for effective interventions and strategies to address and manage their anger.

- **Avoid physical punishment:**

Avoid resorting to physical punishment as a means of discipline. Modern parenting discourages practices like spanking, recognizing its potential to escalate a child's anger rather than effectively addressing the underlying issues.

How to Create an Emotionally Intelligent Household

The family plays a crucial role in shaping a child's self-esteem, confidence, and emotional well-being. Children absorb important lessons by engaging with their parents, observing adult social interactions, and participating in effective communication, especially through active listening. Even at a young age, children begin to grasp emotions on a basic level. Below are the essential elements for creating an emotionally intelligent household.

- **Effective communication:**

Good families communicate and listen to each other. It means not just saying things but also hearing what others say and then adjusting how we talk based on that. In a loving family, everyone talks in a nice way that helps us feel good about ourselves. Listening is important because it helps us understand how others feel. In an emotionally intelligent family, people talk clearly, so it's easy to get what they mean. Asking questions and having conversations make our discussions more interesting and help us connect better. But in families where people don't talk much or don't make things clear, it can be confusing and make it hard to learn good social skills.

- **Don't raise the bar too high or low:**

Toys, books, learning materials, and how we teach them should match what they can understand and do at their age. Even though there are usual things kids learn, each child is special and needs care that suits them. Sometimes, when things don't go well, it's because we expect too much or too little from them. So, it's important to find the right balance for each child.

- **Develop organizational and social skills:**

Teach your kids to be organized, keep things clean, and understand how to act in different situations. You should show how to plan, handle tough times, manage time, and deal with stress. By giving information, guiding, and setting an example, you help build emotional intelligence. If this support is missing, kids might struggle with setting goals and achieving things.

- **Set boundaries:**

In families, it's important to have clear rules that fit each person. Having rules helps everyone express themselves in a strong but not too shy or aggressive way. These rules also create personal dignity and self-respect. They help kids understand what's valuable and what belongs to them. If these rules aren't clear, it might be hard to show respect, follow good manners, and be polite.

Empathy and Connection

Children with ADHD may sometimes appear self-focused and distant due to their inattentiveness. It may seem like they are indifferent to others' thoughts and feelings, as their inattentiveness may be misinterpreted as aloofness. Below are some strategies to cultivate empathy in your child:

- **Be an example:**

As a parent, you play a crucial role in your child's life. Your actions and behavior become a guide for them. When you treat others with respect, show understanding when someone is upset, and celebrate the successes of others, you are imparting valuable lessons in empathy to your child.

- **Celebrate others:**

Acknowledge the achievements of others, including your child's siblings. While you may worry about making your child with ADHD feel bad, it's essential to celebrate the successes of all your children. By recognizing and praising accomplishments, you convey that each child is valued and that their achievements matter.

- **Have conversations about emotions:**

Express what actions bring you joy and explore the things that evoke happiness or sadness for them. Encourage your child to share their feelings and also discuss the emotions of siblings. Take notice of others' feelings in different situations. For instance, in a restaurant, observe and comment on a situation like a child dropping food, saying, "*He just dropped his food. He looks sad.*"

- **Teach them problem-solving techniques:**

Empower your child with problem-solving skills to navigate challenges and setbacks effectively. Teaching them resilience in the face of adversity contributes to the development of empathy as they learn to manage negative emotions and overcome disappointments through practical solutions.

Interactive Element: Emotional Intelligence Self-Assessment

This self-assessment is designed to be a fun and empowering tool for kids with ADHD to explore their emotional world and discover their strengths and areas for growth. Let your child undertake this assessment.

Instructions:

Carefully read each statement and select the answer that describes you the most.

Be honest, and don't worry about getting anything right or wrong - there are no bad answers.

Check Your Mood Meter: How often do you notice your feelings? Circle one:

- a. Always: I'm a total pro at reading my emotions.
- b. Sometimes: I catch myself feeling happy, sad, or angry, but it takes a little effort.
- c. Rarely: My emotions are like a mystery to me!

- **Name Your Feelings:** Can you identify different emotions beyond happy, sad, and mad? List some you know:

_____
_____
_____
_____
_____
_____
_____
_____
_____

- **Emotional Triggers:** What are some things that usually make you feel happy, sad, angry, or frustrated? Write down a few examples for each emotion.

_____
_____
_____
_____
_____
_____
_____

- **Face Reader:** How good are you at guessing how others are feeling by looking at their faces? Circle one:

a. I can crack the code of any expression!
b. I'm getting better at reading faces, but sometimes I need a hint.
c. Faces are just faces to me.

- **Body Language Detective:** Can you pick up on clues about someone's feelings from their body language? List some examples:

_____
_____
_____
_____
_____
_____

- **Empathy Challenge:** Imagine a friend is feeling sad because they lost a game. How would you comfort them? Write down what you would say or do.

_____
_____

_____
_____
_____
_____
_____

- **Cool Down Techniques:** When you're feeling overwhelmed by strong emotions, what do you do to calm down? List some of your coping mechanisms:

_____
_____
_____
_____
_____

- **Communication Master:** How do you express your feelings to others healthily? Circle one:

a. I talk it out: I tell people exactly how I feel, even if it's tough.
b. I show, don't tell: I use my actions and words to express myself.

c. I keep it bottled up: Sharing my feelings feels too risky.

- **Positive Choices:** When you're feeling angry or frustrated, do you make choices you're proud of later? Circle one:

a. Yes, always: I can control my emotions and make good decisions.
b. Sometimes: I try to make good choices, but it's not always easy.
c. No, not really: My emotions get the best of me sometimes.

For kids with ADHD, emotional intelligence is a superpower. It helps understand, express, and manage emotions, reducing meltdowns and improving relationships. Creating an emotionally intelligent household involves effective communication, appropriate expectations, organizational skills, clear boundaries, and nurturing empathy.

While developing emotional intelligence, hyper-focus can be a challenge. That is why the next chapter will explore how to leverage the power of hyper-focus in developing your child's emotional intelligence.

Key Takeaways

- For kids with ADHD, cultivating emotional intelligence is a superpower, helping them navigate intense emotions and build fulfilling relationships.

- Self-awareness, self-regulation, social skills, empathy, and motivation are essential components of emotional intelligence for kids with ADHD.

- Teaching children to create space, notice, name, and accept their emotions empowers them to take control and navigate complex feelings effectively.

- Techniques such as limiting screen time, recognizing anger as a signal, and avoiding physical punishment contribute to managing anger in children with ADHD.

- Fostering empathy involves being an example, celebrating others' successes, having conversations about emotions, and teaching problem-solving techniques.

- A self-assessment engages children in exploring their emotional world and evaluating their mood awareness, emotional triggers, and coping mechanisms.

"Just as every superhero uses their powers for good, your kind words can become someone's superpower!" - **Inspired by the heroes among us**

Hello, Amazing Parents and Super Readers!

Did you know that some people with ADHD have powers like quick thinking and lots of energy? That's super cool, isn't it? Michael Phelps, the swimming legend, didn't let ADHD slow him down. Nope! He splashed his way to 28 Olympic medals. Wowzah! He used his ADHD superpowers to zoom through the water and become the most decorated Olympian ever.

So, what does this have to do with reviews?

Well, your words have power, too – they can lift someone and make them feel like they can swim across the ocean!

Here's a big, superhero-sized question for you:

Would you be awesome and give a boost to someone you've never met, just like a secret sidekick?

Who could this be?

It's someone who's a lot like you were once. Maybe a little unsure, wanting to make a big splash in the world of parenting, and looking for the super tips and tricks to help their super kid.

Our super mission is to share the secrets of **PARENTING SUPERKIDS WITH ADHD** with all the moms and dads out there. Everything I do is zapped with that mission. But reaching the whole world? That's a big adventure, and I need you, the incredible parents and readers, to join the super team.

Now, it's true, a lot of folks decide which book to read based on what other super readers say. So, here's my super ask for all the parents who have kids with ADHD:

Could you zoom over and leave a super review for this book?

It's faster than a speeding bullet (well, almost) and doesn't cost a dime. Your review could be the cape that helps another parent of a super kid with ADHD fly!

Your super words could help...

...another family feels like heroes.

...another parent discovers their super strength.

...another super kid unleashes their incredible power.

...and maybe, just maybe, start another amazing adventure.

To send your super review flying, it's super easy and super quick – just a zap and you're done!

Scan this super QR code to leave your super review:

If you're ready to join the League of Extraordinary Parents, I'm super excited to welcome you. You're part of the team now!

I can't wait to show you how you can navigate the adventure of ADHD with the super strategies coming up next.

A super thanks from the deepest part of my superhero heart. And now, let's zoom back into the action!

- Your biggest cheerleader, Phoenix J. Waldren

P.S. - Super fact: When you share something super valuable, it makes you a superhero in someone else's story. If you think this book could be a super tool for another parent or super kid, why not pass it on and spread the super vibes?

Chapter Six

Hyper-Focus: The Secret Lair of Concentration

"Failure is not the end of your story; it is the start of your new comeback story"

- ***Captain America.***

Most of the time, when people hear the term "attention deficit disorder," what comes to mind is that people with it have difficulty focusing, but that's a bit misleading. ADHD is more about regulating attention than lacking it. People with ADHD struggle with mundane tasks but can hyper-focus on things that interest them, leading to the misconception that they "can focus when they want to." However, focusing is complex, requiring the right mix of personal interest, stimulation, and reward, making it challenging for those with ADHD to engage in less interesting tasks.

Lower dopamine levels in the brain, particularly in the prefrontal cortex, which plays a crucial role in attention, focus, and motivation, are the scientific explanation for hyper-focus in ADHD. However, during hyperfocus, dopamine seems to be released in a more concentrated and sustained manner within specific brain regions. This targeted dopamine release activates the brain's reward system, creating a sense of pleasure and satisfaction associated with the hyper-focused activity. This positive feedback loop further fuels focus and engagement.

However, that isn't something to worry about because you can learn how to leverage your child's hyper-focus and focus in the right direction. But before we delve into that, let's look at some hyper-focus triggers.

- **Interest**: Hyper-focus is often triggered by activities that genuinely spark curiosity, and excitement, or hold personal meaning, such as painting, coding, writing, or playing a musical instrument.

- **Challenge**: New experiences, complex tasks, or activities that require problem-solving can activate the brain's reward system, reinforcing the focus loop and triggering hyper-focus.

- **Sensory Preferences:** Some children with ADHD find specific sensory experiences, like listening to particular music or working in specific environments

- **Deadlines:** The pressure of approaching deadlines or the need to deliver can trigger hyper-focus.

- **Structured Environments:** Organized workspaces, clear instructions, and well-defined goals provide a framework for hyper-focus to take hold, reducing cognitive load and facilitating concentration.

Channeling Hyper-Focus Productively

As said earlier, hyper-focus can make your child find it challenging to focus on mundane tasks while they focus extensively on one of their choices. So, how do you help your child to navigate these complexities? Here are some tips that can help them to channel their hyper-focus to enhance productivity.

- **Remove distractions:**

Eliminating potential disturbances is crucial when your child has a task to complete and is prone to distractions. Encourage them to move their phone to a different room or switch it off, and contemplate blocking distracting websites on their computer until they finish the task. By removing these common distractions, your child might find it easier to channel their hyper-focus into the task at hand. Distractions vary from person to person, and what might distract one person could be completely different for another.

For instance, while some people might find background podcasts or videos distracting, people with ADHD may discover that such stimuli help them navigate through less engaging tasks. Alternatively, your child might identify distractions in unexpected places, like having an excessive number of pens on their desk, leading to activities such as playing with the pens, arranging them, or repeatedly taking off and putting on the lids.

- **Promote creativity:**

To harness hyper-focus more effectively, encourage your child to infuse creativity into routine tasks. Help them explore ways to transform mundane work into dynamic activities that align with their interests. For instance:

- Turn notes or flashcards into a musical experience and create a dance routine to aid memorization.

- Visualize concepts by drawing diagrams, charts, and illustrations instead of relying solely on written paragraphs.

- Transform a paper into a play, movie pitch, or comic book for a fresh perspective.

- Add visual interest to worksheets using colorful pens, highlighters, and different fonts.

- Enhance presentations with multimedia elements like videos, animations, and interactive features.

- Develop mnemonic songs, rhymes, or raps for vocabulary words to facilitate recall.

- Act out problem-solving scenarios physically or use props as needed.

- Infuse personal stories and examples into their work to make it more engaging.

By tapping into imagination and talents, your child can turn routine tasks into enjoyable, creative activities that capture and maintain their attention. Let their intrinsic interests guide them in making work both fun and engaging.

- **Use Pomodoro Technique:**

Introduce the Pomodoro technique to your child as a helpful method for concentrated work. Guide them to set a timer for 25 minutes, dedicating that time solely to a specific task like homework or chores. After this focused period, encourage a 5-minute break. Repeat this cycle with subsequent timers for effective bursts of attention.

For added engagement, explore Pomodoro videos on YouTube with diverse themes and background music. These videos eliminate the need for manual reminders; simply press play, and the video will guide your child through the focused and break intervals.

Remember, shorter time blocks are particularly beneficial for individuals with ADHD. Trying to sustain focus for 2-3 hours can be challenging, so breaking it into manageable intervals sets the stage for success.

- **Exercise before tasks:**

Encourage your child to integrate physical activity before tackling tasks to trigger hyper-focus. Engaging in exercise, especially aerobic activities, releases neurotransmitters like dopamine, enhancing motivation and attention. Here are some suggestions:

- Let them take a 15–30-minute walk or jog, favoring aerobic exercises.

- They can try High-Intensity Interval Training with activities like jumping jacks, squats, and lunges.

- They can consider a focused yoga routine, including grounding poses like planks.

- Shoot hoops, kick a soccer ball, or jump rope for 5-10 minutes.

Select activities your child enjoys to make this routine more appealing. Hydrate afterward, as a mini-workout can optimize their mental state for hyper-focus. Experiment with different movements to discover what works best before concentration-demanding tasks.

- **Strategic Task Sequencing:**

Help your child strategically plan their day by encouraging them to tackle fewer exciting tasks first to avoid hyper-focusing on fun activities. Completing mundane chores early leaves enjoyable tasks as a rewarding option for the remaining time. Consider these suggestions:

- Save enjoyable activities as a reward for later in the day after completing fewer exciting tasks.

- Avoid overwhelming chores; break them down. For example, wash a manageable number of dishes instead of tackling the entire pile.

- Set short timers, like two minutes, for tasks. Wash as much as possible within that time, allowing a natural break afterward.

By adopting these strategies, your child can navigate their tasks more effectively and avoid the challenge of switching away from engaging activities once started.

Creating the Right Environment for Concentration and Organization

When helping children with ADHD to leverage their hyper-focus, creating the right environment is important. Below are tips to help you create a conducive environment for concentration and organization for your child.

- **Dedicated workspace:**

Establishing a designated and appealing work area is crucial for creating an environment conducive to concentration for ADHD children. Ensure this space is tailored to minimize distractions, free from items like TVs or video games, and equipped with essential supplies such as a desk, a comfortable chair, and necessary school materials. Use vibrant colors and visually stimulating elements to make the space attractive, which can promote focus and spark creativity.

- **Create a distraction-free zone:**

We can't emphasize this point enough. Make a calm space for your ADHD child to concentrate by cutting down on distractions. Turn off background TVs and reduce loud noises from other rooms. If needed, use blackout curtains to block light and sound barriers to minimize noise. This creates a peaceful environment, helping your child focus without interruptions.

- **Visual organization:**

Help your child with ADHD by using visual organization like shelves, boxes, and labels to keep their space neat. Shelves are great for books and school stuff, while boxes can stash toys. Labels show what's inside. Let your child pick colors or decorate labels; it makes them feel involved and responsible for keeping things in order.

- **Structured routine:**

Set up a daily routine with dedicated time slots for various activities, like meals, schoolwork, breaks, and play. Display the schedule prominently, ideally in your child's work area, for easy reference. Ensure a good balance between activities, incorporating relaxation and play to prevent over-stimulation and maintain a structured routine.

- **Visual Aid for Time Management:**

Support your child's time management with visual aids and timers. Employ a visual clock with colored markers to highlight key daily events, like bedtime or homework time. Utilize visual timers or mobile apps to set activity time limits, enhancing independent time management skills.

- **Encourage planning:**

Empower your child by involving them in activity planning. Have them create to-do lists or calendars to instill a sense of control and responsibility. Assist in prioritizing tasks and setting achievable goals. Introduce fun elements like checking off completed tasks or using stickers to track progress, reinforcing a sense of accomplishment and motivation for consistent routines.

Positive Impact of Hyper-Focus

We have explored how to channel hyper-focus for productivity. However, you may wonder why doing that is so important. Well, hyper-focus has its advantages, and that's why you need to know how to channel it in the right direction. Here are some positive impacts of hyper-focus:

- **Exceptional Concentration:** During hyper-focus, children can exhibit an intense and prolonged focus on a specific task or activity, leading to increased productivity and efficiency.

- **Enhanced Creativity:** The heightened concentration in hyper-focus can stimulate creative thinking and problem-solving.

  This would allow kids to explore innovative ideas and solutions.

- **Increased Productivity:** The ability to immerse deeply in a task can result in higher productivity levels, enabling children to accomplish more within a concentrated period.

- **Task Completion:** Hyper-focus can contribute to a greater likelihood of completing tasks and assignments, especially those that align with your child's interests or passions.

- **Skill Mastery:** When hyper-focused on a particular skill or activity, children may experience accelerated learning and skill development, potentially leading to mastery in specific areas.

Balancing Focus with Flexibility

Many children thrive with consistent routines, providing comfort and predictability for both parents and kids. Establishing daily routines helps reduce the fear of the unknown, a common trigger for tantrums in children facing constant change. This is particularly valuable during transitions, such as giving up a bottle, starting at a new daycare, changing schools, relocating to a new city, or making new friends. Routines contribute to a sense of stability by easing anxiety and fostering comfort and safety in a child's evolving world.

Moreover, routines play a role in teaching children self-control and internal regulation. Routines assist in creating constructive habits and guide children in managing themselves and their surroundings, offering not only a sense of safety but also important developmental benefits.

While routines offer comfort and teach self-control, an excessive focus on consistency can lead to undue anxiety and unhealthy rigidity. Striking a balance between routine and flexibility is crucial to acknowledging life's unpredictability. Flexibility in parenting allows room for mistakes, learning, and growth within the family.

A flexible approach emphasizes that the family operates as a team, fostering a sense that everyone's voice matters. Allowing children to make minor decisions, like choosing a restaurant for a routine Friday night order-in, promotes openness and adaptability. This adaptability is crucial for children to navigate life's changes, fostering resilience in the face of challenges.

Flexibility not only makes parenting easier but also acknowledges the trial-and-error nature of parenting. Being open to change when routines aren't effective or when mistakes occur allows for continuous learning and growth. Embracing flexibility enables parents to adjust their strategies, ensuring they meet the unique needs of each child.

Parenting involves a lot of experimentation. Rather than sticking to a single approach, it's liberating to explore different methods and perspectives. Not every strategy will fit your family, and that's perfectly fine. Embracing an open mindset, being willing to learn, and evolving as a parent enable you to connect with each of your kids in a way that suits them best.

So, how do you find the right balance? To find the right balance for your family, it's crucial to align decisions with your core beliefs. Ask yourself whether a deviation from the routine remains true to your fundamental principles. If the answer is yes, incorporating flexibility may be beneficial. For example, if extending bedtime on a Saturday night for a family activity aligns with your goal of enjoying recreation together, a flexible approach to bedtime could be valuable. Staying mindful of your goals and core beliefs and consistently prioritizing them allows you to navigate the balance between routine and flexibility that suits your family.

Hyper-Focus Discovery Activities

Below are some activities that can help your child with hyper-focus:

- **Coin Game:**

The Coin Game is a favorite among parents for its positive impact on memory, sequencing, attention, and concentration, while kids find it engaging due to its fast-paced and enjoyable nature.

To play, gather a small assortment of coins, a cardboard sheet for covering, and a timer or stopwatch. Select five coins (e.g., three pennies and two nickels) and arrange them in a sequence. Instruct your child to carefully observe the arrangement, then cover the coins with the cardboard. Start the timer and ask them to replicate the pattern using coins from the pile. Record the time taken and its accuracy. If the pattern isn't correct, encourage them to persist until they are successful.

You can enhance the challenge by introducing various coins like pennies, nickels, dimes, quarters, and half dollars. As you progress, you'll likely observe improvements in your child's concentration and sequencing skills, making it a rewarding experience for both of you.

- **Relaxation and Positive Imagery:**

Pairing basic relaxation methods like deep breathing with positive visual imagery can enhance the brain's ability to acquire or refine skills. Mentally rehearsing activities, such as a golf swing, register in the brain similarly to actual practice, resulting in tangible improvement.

For children with ADHD, envisioning scenarios like attentiveness in class or managing teasing can influence their behavior positively at school. Harnessing creativity, you and your child can explore these techniques together.

- **Mind-Body Integration:**

Try this exercise: have your child sit in a chair without moving, and time how long they can maintain stillness. With consistent practice over weeks, you'll likely observe progress. This activity reinforces neural connections between the brain and body, fostering enhanced self-control in your child.

- **Memory and Concentration Games:**

Engaging in children's games like Simon Says can be a fun way to boost memory and concentration. These games, which involve remembering picture locations or sequences of visual and auditory stimuli, exercise and challenge brain circuits. Regular play strengthens connections and enhances overall cognitive function. Additionally, you can explore numerous free online games on platforms like PBS Kids, Fun Brain, and Mr. Nussbaum to further improve concentration and memory skills.

- **Crossword Puzzles and Picture Puzzles:**

Simple yet effective, crossword puzzles prove to be valuable tools for enhancing attention to words and sequencing abilities in kids with ADHD. Similarly, picture puzzles, where younger children identify "wrong" elements in a picture or search for hidden objects, contribute to improving attention and concentration skills.

- **Story-Based Games:**

Engage your child with story-based games using a good storybook and imagination. After reading a short story, quiz your child on the content or ask them to predict what might happen next after reading a paragraph. Maintain connections to the original story, taking turns to build on the narrative. These games aid in developing working memory, concentration, logic, and a sense of humor.

- **Paddle Ball:**

Rediscover the classic paddle ball game with your child. Use a wooden paddle with a rubber ball attached to a rubber band. Begin by bouncing the ball downward and progress to bouncing it upward as mastery develops. Track your child's progress and encourage them to extend the bouncing duration. For older kids, discuss setting records as a motivational challenge.

- **Dancing Sequence Games:**

Explore different versions suitable for your child's age and preferences, playable on platforms like Xbox and Wii. Invest in the corresponding dance mat for your gaming system. These games enhance concentration, processing speed, planning, sequencing, and motor integration. As a bonus, they offer a fun way to incorporate aerobic exercise into your child's routine.

In conclusion, ADHD isn't a lack of attention but a challenge in regulating it. Hyper-focus, a unique aspect, stems from lower dopamine levels, creating a positive feedback loop that intensifies engagement. Even though hyper-focus can be a challenge, it can be channeled to yield exceptional concentration, enhanced creativity, increased productivity, improved task completion, and skill mastery.

In the next chapter, we will learn how to harness the power of routine and structure to support your child's hyper-focus.

Key Takeaways

- Leveraging hyper-focus can lead to exceptional concentration, enhanced creativity, increased productivity, improved task completion, and skill mastery.
- Activities that genuinely interest, challenge, align with sensory preferences, involve deadlines, or occur in structured environments can trigger hyper-focus.
- Establishing a dedicated workspace, minimizing distractions, employing visual organization, following

structured routines, and using visual aids for time management are essential for concentration.
- While routines provide stability, flexibility is crucial for adapting to life's changes, teaching adaptability, and making parenting more manageable.
- Engaging in activities like the Coin Game, mind-body integration, picture puzzles, story-based games, paddle balls, and dancing sequence games can enhance concentration.

Chapter Seven

The Rhythm of Routine – Structuring Success for ADHD Minds

"It's not who I am underneath, but what I do that defines me."

- Batman

Imagine you are working in an organization, and you have no idea what you will do the next day. Your boss tells you what to do when you resume work every day. How would you feel? It can be tiring and frustrating, right? Not having an idea of what the next day would look like. That is a similar thing that happens when children, especially those with ADHD, don't have a routine. As a parent, you already know that your child has challenges paying attention; I think it is unfair to do things spontaneously and expect them to adjust.

In the hustle of daily life, your focus on completing tasks might overshadow the importance of strategically planning your day for the benefit of your child. Creating predictability in your daily routines is crucial for your child's well-being. Knowing what to expect and understanding how you will respond provides a sense of safety for your child, smoothing their mood and reducing the likelihood of meltdowns. When children face uncertainty about daily expectations, anxiety rises, leading to increased demands on their time.

Establishing predictability through consistent routines fosters a positive environment, aiding your child's emotional regulation and overall growth. The developing brain thrives on repetition, making a predictable environment less stressful and more conducive to learning. Embracing consistency in your responses eliminates the guessing game for your child, offering them security and benefiting both you and your child in the long run.

To start, you should introduce consistent strategies at home, creating an environment that feels predictable. For instance, having a morning routine is important as it helps your kids prepare for the day. Below are tips for having an effective morning routine:

- **Give them extra time:**

Most people, unless they're natural morning enthusiasts, often struggle to get moving in the early hours. This challenge becomes more significant for children with ADHD, given the common association between ADHD and sleep difficulties. Adults with ADHD may resort to multiple alarms to combat this struggle.

As a parent aiming to assist your child with ADHD in the morning, consider incorporating extra time for the waking-up process. One effective strategy involves gently waking your child 30 minutes to an hour before their intended wake-up time, allowing for a gradual transition into the day.

Moreover, if getting your child out of bed remains a considerable challenge, discussing the timing of their ADHD medication with your doctor could be beneficial. Administering medication, a bit earlier in the morning enables it to take effect as your child slowly awakens and starts their day. This thoughtful approach recognizes the unique needs of individuals with ADHD and tailors' strategies to foster a more manageable morning routine.

- **Maximize the night before:**

Streamline your mornings by acknowledging the perpetual time crunch that often characterizes the early hours. Most of us have experienced the rush and time scarcity that define mornings, creating a sense of urgency to meet work and school schedules. To effectively navigate a morning routine, it becomes crucial to allocate some tasks to the preceding evening.

Recognizing the limited time available in the morning, it's practical to tackle specific preparations the night before. While addressing every aspect of your morning routine in advance may not be feasible, you can manage key tasks. Consider activities such as preparing your kids' lunches, organizing their school bags, and laying out their clothes.

Despite the fatigue that typically accompanies the end of the day, optimizing your evening, especially after your kids are asleep, can significantly enhance your morning routine. Utilizing this time efficiently allows you to handle essential tasks for the upcoming morning, contributing to a smoother start to the day. This strategic approach not only saves time but also reduces the potential for frustration during your morning routine.

- **Remove distraction:**

Distractions have the uncanny ability to throw off schedules and plunge mornings into chaos. Amidst the flurry of activities like waking up, showering, dressing, and grabbing a quick meal, every moment is precious. To ensure a smooth morning routine, it's imperative to eliminate all unnecessary distractions.

If your children express a desire to watch morning TV or indulge in a quick video game session, evaluate whether these activities contribute to the goal of efficiently leaving the house. If not, it's time to cut them out and refocus on the fundamental objective of preparing everyone and facilitating a seamless departure.

Approach your morning routine as a sequential series of tasks, each demanding attention and completion. Waking up, getting dressed, eating, collecting items for work and school, and finally heading out the door should be the primary focus. While the specifics of these tasks may vary based on your routine, the overarching principle remains a singular focus on task completion and progression to the next.

Distractions only serve to impede progress and hinder task accomplishment. Save unproductive distractions until later in the day, perhaps during after-school hours. If your kids veer toward distractions during the morning rush, gently redirect their attention, emphasizing that such activities can wait for a more suitable time. Reserve your mornings for purposeful activities that propel you closer to the overarching goal of ensuring everyone reaches their destinations on time.

- **Prioritize a healthy breakfast:**

To ensure an effective ADHD morning routine, prioritize a wholesome and nutritious breakfast. Although mornings can be overwhelming, resist the temptation to overlook breakfast. Instead, make it a priority for everyone in the family.

Despite potential challenges, creative solutions can integrate breakfast seamlessly into your routine. Consider preparing breakfast the night before, getting an early start on breakfast before your kids wake up, or involving your kids in the process of making their breakfast.

Regardless of the approach, the key is to emphasize healthy, non-processed food choices. Avoiding processed cereals with additives and sugars is essential, as these can exacerbate ADHD symptoms. Choose nourishing options like fruits and nuts, a revitalizing smoothie, or a wholesome omelet instead of sugary cereals or pastries.

By giving precedence to a healthy breakfast in your morning routine, you not only ensure your kids start their day with the energy they need but also contribute to managing their symptoms through a balanced diet.

- **Distribute tasks:**

In a household with limited space, juggling morning tasks can be a real challenge, especially when there's only one bathroom or kitchen. When everyone can't simultaneously brush their teeth or complete their morning routine, it becomes essential to assign each child their own routine and tasks. Once the routines are defined, the key is to stagger them, ensuring each family member tackles different activities at different times.

> *"Life doesn't give us purpose. We give life purpose." –* **The Flash**

To implement this approach effectively, establish distinct structures for each person in the family. Consider having one child eat breakfast while another gets ready for school, and then switch roles if you have multiple children. To maintain organization and guide everyone in the right direction, craft an ADHD morning routine chart. This chart can feature each person's name alongside the sequence of activities and tasks they need to complete.

Dividing and staggering tasks helps prevent congestion at any particular point in the process, minimizing the potential for arguments. Furthermore, separating kids into different areas of the house during their routines can proactively avoid conflicts before they even arise.

After School Routine

We all know that children with ADHD thrive on consistency, but maintaining it can be a challenge, especially when it comes to homework. The key is to create a structured routine that not only reduces battles but also enhances productivity and academic performance. These tips will help:

- Kickstart the homework session at the same time every day. This regularity helps your child develop a habit, making it easier to transition into homework mode.

- Many children with ADHD benefit from adult supervision during homework time. Whether they're sitting nearby or actively assisting, your presence can boost their focus and productivity.

- ADHD traits like distractibility and restlessness can lead to mental fatigue. Integrate short, frequent breaks into the study session, allowing your child to move around and recharge. These pauses can combat boredom and frustration, fostering a more sustainable focus.

- Make homework a rewarding experience by offering a fun activity as a post-homework treat. Knowing that an enjoyable activity awaits can motivate your child to tackle assignments with greater enthusiasm and diligence.

By implementing these strategies, you can create a supportive homework environment that empowers your child to tackle academic challenges with confidence and consistency.

Dinner Routine

In this era of digital distractions, the age-old tradition of gathering around the dinner table remains not just beneficial but, in fact, essential. Despite our busy schedules, dedicating about 20 minutes to a shared meal holds immense value. Here's why maintaining a consistent dinnertime schedule is worth the effort:

- **Cultivating Strong Connections:** The dinner table has been a hub for family bonding for centuries. By consistently gathering for meals, you foster strong connections among family members. It's a dedicated time to share experiences, joys, and challenges, enhancing the family's connection.

- **Quality Social Interaction:** Mealtimes offer a unique opportunity for quality social interaction. Set aside the screens and leave the stresses of work or school behind. Engage in conversations that go beyond the surface, allowing each family member's voice to be heard.

- **Inclusive Decision-Making:** During dinner, important family matter and plans can be discussed with input from everyone. This inclusive approach strengthens the sense of responsibility within the family.

- **Encouraging Responsibility:** Simple acts like children setting the table and participating in the cleanup afterward instill a sense of responsibility. These shared responsibilities contribute to a cooperative family environment, teaching valuable life skills along the way.

Bedtime Routine

Bedtime can often be a battleground for parents, especially when it comes to children with ADHD, who may find the prospect of sleep less than thrilling. However, research underscores the importance of consistent bedtime routines in promoting better sleep habits. Here's how you can create a bedtime routine that eases your child into sleep while keeping them engaged:

- Offer a light, nutritious snack like an apple or cheese on a rice cake. This not only helps stave off hunger but also signals to the body that it's time to wind down for the night.

- Engage in quiet, low-key activities, such as playing a calming game or reading a book together. These activities not only help distract from any lingering excitement but also promote relaxation, making it easier for your child to transition to sleep.

- Establish a sweet and personal nightly lights-out ritual that your child looks forward to. This could be anything from a special bedtime story to a few minutes of quiet cuddle time. The key is to make it consistent and comforting.

- Aim to get your child into bed at the same time each evening, even on weekends. Consistency reinforces the body's internal clock, making it easier for your child to fall asleep and wake up refreshed.

By incorporating these elements into your bedtime routine, you can help your child unwind, settle into sleep more easily, and enjoy a restful night's sleep, setting the stage for a positive start to the next day.

The Key Elements of a Successful Routine

While working on a routine for your child with ADHD, it is important to incorporate key elements to ensure effectiveness. Here are key elements to ensure a successful routine for your child.

- **Involve your kids in decision-making:**

Encourage your children to actively participate in decision-making to establish a routine that suits their preferences. When children have a say in the choices shaping their routine, it not only sparks enthusiasm but also fosters a sense of empowerment. Providing options and letting them voice their preferences not only makes tasks more appealing but also boosts their confidence. When children believe they have a role in shaping their daily activities, they develop a sense of responsibility, making them more likely to tackle tasks independently and with a positive mindset. Involving them in decision-making becomes a powerful tool for building a routine that suits both their needs and your parenting goals.

- **Be realistic:**

Ensure your routine is realistic for your kids by considering the time required for each task. Assess the duration needed for every activity and establish realistic priorities. If a routine feels overly demanding or time-constrained, children might struggle to comply. Identify essential tasks and prioritize them, allowing flexibility for "extra" activities. By acknowledging realistic time constraints, you reduce potential tension and negative emotions. A manageable routine not only enhances adherence but also creates a positive environment, making it more likely for your children to successfully navigate their daily tasks.

- **Clarity is key:**

Ensure your children adhere to the routine by providing clear explanations. Make sure they understand each step and its timing. Clearly outline the tasks and their requirements. Precision is key when giving instructions; break down each process and specify the necessary actions for each task. By offering clear explanations, you empower your children to comprehend and follow the routine effectively. This clarity reduces confusion and enhances their ability to independently manage and complete tasks within the established routine.

- **Write routine:**

Help your children stay on track by writing out the routine. Just like your to-do list, children benefit from visual reminders. Document and display the routine in a location that is easily accessible. Break down the tasks into manageable groups, ideally three to five at a time, to avoid overwhelming them. For younger children, combine written instructions with visual aids to help them better understand and visualize each activity.

This dual approach, incorporating both written and pictorial elements, enhances comprehension and makes the routine more accessible for your children.

- **Be supportive:**

Support your child throughout the adjustment to new routines, recognizing that change takes time. Instead of expecting instant transformations, celebrate small improvements along the way. Remind your child gently, both verbally and by directing their attention to the written schedule. If they need help, be readily available. Always acknowledge and appreciate the effort they've put in, stressing that you applaud their attempt to stick to the schedule, even if perfection isn't immediate.

Incorporating Flexibility Within Structure

When it comes to organizing tasks and creating schedules for your child with ADHD, it's common to encounter challenges, especially when things don't go as planned. Many parents' express frustration when a task takes longer than expected or when unexpected events disrupt the schedule. While it's true that rigid plans can be difficult to stick to, there are ways to build flexibility into your approach. Here's some practical advice on how to create to-do lists and plans that allow for adjustments and flexibility when needed.

- **Have a master to-do list:**

It's a great idea to start by creating a master to-do list that includes all the tasks your child needs to complete, along with their due dates. This list functions as a central hub for managing all tasks, ensuring crucial tasks don't slip through the cracks.

To make it even more organized, you can categorize tasks into different groups. For example, you might have categories like one-time tasks, which are things that only need to be done once; recurring tasks, which are tasks that need to be done regularly; and separate categories for personal and work-related tasks. This categorization can assist your child in prioritizing their tasks and concentrating on the most important ones.

- **Time for each task:**

It's essential to map out a plan for when each task will be completed to ensure they don't get overlooked. One effective way to do this is by using an hour-by-hour calendar, either on paper or electronically, such as Google Calendar.

You can approach this in two ways. First, you can list each task individually on the calendar, estimating how much time each one will take. Alternatively, you can organize tasks into categories and allocate specific blocks of time to complete tasks within each category. This helps your child visualize their schedule and ensures they allocate enough time for each task without feeling overwhelmed.

- **Don't overload:**

It's crucial not to overload your child's schedule with back-to-back tasks. Instead, leave some breathing room by keeping two or three blocks of time, each lasting 15 to 30 minutes, free from scheduled activities.

Additionally, incorporate shorter, 5-minute slots throughout the day, ideally spaced in the morning, midday, and evening. These brief intervals serve as opportunities to adjust the plan if needed and to plan for the following day. This flexibility allows your child to adapt to unexpected changes and maintain a sense of control over their schedule.

- **Adjust to changes:**

When unexpected events disrupt your child's schedule, consider the following strategies for adjustment:

a. **Maintain Order:**

If a single event causes a delay, continue completing the tasks in their original order. Take advantage of any reserved 15- to 30-minute blocks to compensate for lost time. This approach is helpful when tasks take longer than anticipated or when unexpected interruptions occur.

b. **Skip and Reschedule:**

In cases were staying on track is challenging, consider skipping the next scheduled item to maintain overall alignment with the plan. During the next planning block, allocate a new time to address the skipped task.

c. **Prioritize Critical Tasks:**

Prioritize the remaining tasks scheduled before the next planning block. Start with the most important ones to ensure essential activities are accomplished efficiently. This strategic approach helps maintain focus and productivity despite unforeseen disruptions.

d. Update your list:

When plans change, you must check and update your list of missed activities. During your designated planning periods, follow these steps:

i. Reschedule Uncompleted Tasks:

Allocate new times to complete tasks that were not addressed according to the original plan. Adjust the schedule as needed to accommodate these tasks effectively.

ii. Address New Items:

If new tasks arise, assess their urgency and importance. Schedule them accordingly within the existing day's plan, adjusting other tasks if required. Alternatively, reserve time on another day to address these new items comprehensively.

iii. Mindful Transition:

At the beginning or end of a planning period, let your child take a moment to relax and rejuvenate. Let them Engage in brief mindfulness exercises, listen to guided visual imagery or calming music, or indulge in another time-limited activity that promotes mental clarity and focus. This brief break prepares them to transition back to work with renewed energy and concentration.

Routine-building workshop

Here's a structured sample schedule to help organize daily activities for a child with ADHD:

Morning Routine:

- **7:00 a.m.:** Wake your child up with some playful energy to kick-start the day.

- **7:05 a.m.:** Follow a checklist for getting ready, encouraging your child to complete tasks independently.

- **7:20 a.m.:** Provide a simple breakfast with limited options to minimize decision-making stress.

- **7:45 a.m.:** Brush teeth together to ensure thoroughness and efficiency.

- **7:55 a.m.:** Help your child with final preparations like zipping up jackets and putting on shoes.

- **8:00 a.m.:** Head out the door to start the day.

After-School Homework Routine:

- **3:00 p.m.:** Offer a snack and time to relax after school.
- **3:30 p.m.:** Settle your child into a designated homework area with all necessary materials.
- **3:35 – 4:30 p.m.:** Allow your child to work independently with periodic check-ins and breaks.
- **4:25 p.m.:** Review completed work together, offering praise and guidance without taking over.

Dinner Preparation Routine:

- **6:00 p.m.:** Begin food preparation with an organized approach to streamline mealtime.
- **6:15 p.m.:** Involve the kids in setting the table and assigning specific tasks for accountability.
- **6:30 p.m.:** Let the kids handle beverage pouring to encourage participation.
- **6:45 p.m.:** Serve dinner at the table and initiate conversation by sharing highlights of the day.

Bedtime Routine:

- **8:00 p.m.:** Allow time for a relaxing bath or quiet activity to wind down.
- **8:20 p.m.:** Complete the essential bedtime tasks—drying off, brushing teeth, and using the bathroom.
- **8:30 p.m.:** Change into pajamas and tidy up toys to signal bedtime.
- **8:40 p.m.:** Read together to foster a calm and cozy atmosphere.
- **8:55 p.m.:** Help your child settle into bed, reflecting on the day and expressing affection before saying goodnight.

In conclusion, routines provide a roadmap, offering a clear path for your child to follow and reducing the anxiety that comes with unpredictability. Even while maintaining a routine, flexibility is crucial, allowing room for adjustments when things don't go as planned. Whether it's rescheduling tasks or prioritizing critical activities, maintaining order amidst disruptions ensures a smoother transition back on track.

In the next chapter, you will see how nutrition not only conquers hunger but also plays a massive role in enhancing cognitive function, especially for a child with ADHD.

Key Takeaways

- Actively involve your child in decision-making for their routine.
- Set achievable goals within the routine, considering the time needed for each task, to avoid unnecessary tension and stress.
- Ensure your child understands and adheres to the routine by clearly explaining it, breaking down tasks, and specifying actions.
- Write out the routine, display it prominently, and combine it with visual aids to help your child comprehend and follow the schedule effectively.
- Assist your child through the adjustment period, celebrate small advancements, and acknowledge effort, emphasizing progress over perfection.
- Build flexibility into the routine, allowing for adjustments when unexpected events occur, maintaining order, and preventing undue stress.

Chapter Eight

Fueling a Superheroes Fire – Nutrition and Exercise for the ADHD Brain

"Being a super spy requires agility, strength, and endurance. Your mission may not be covert, but your nutrition should be a top priority."

- Black Widow

When discussing managing ADHD, people rarely talk about diet and exercise. Why? Maybe because they feel that there is little nutrition and exercise that can be done to help children with ADHD, but that's a big lie. While diet and exercise aren't magic cures for ADHD, they are superpowers in disguise, fueling your child's focus, unleashing their energy, and managing their minds. As we proceed, we will explore how you can leverage the benefits of nutrition and exercise for your ADHD child.

The ADHD Diet

Crafting an ADHD diet isn't a one-size-fits-all approach; it varies based on your child's requirements. It encompasses the foods they consume and any nutritional supplements they incorporate. Ideally, their dietary habits should optimize brain function and alleviate symptoms such as restlessness and lack of focus.

There are diverse strategies for addressing your child's ADHD symptoms through diet. They include:

- **Overall Nutrition:**

    This approach acknowledges that certain foods they eat may exacerbate or reduce their symptoms. Additionally, it recognizes the potential benefits of incorporating specific nutrients that might be lacking in their diet.

- **Supplementation Diet:**

  In this plan, you add vitamins, minerals, or other nutrients to compensate for potential deficiencies. Advocates of supplementation diets suggest that inadequate intake of certain nutrients could contribute to their symptom manifestation.

- **Elimination Diets:**

  These diets involve excluding foods or ingredients you believe may trigger specific behaviors or worsen your child's symptoms. By identifying and eliminating potential culprits, you aim to mitigate the impact of these dietary factors on your child's ADHD symptoms.

  Adopting a diet beneficial for brain health is likely to positively impact ADHD. For your child, consider incorporating:

- **High-Protein Diet:**

  Include beans, cheese, eggs, meat, and nuts as good protein sources, especially during breakfast and after-school snacks. This might enhance concentration and potentially extend the effectiveness of ADHD medications.

- **More Complex Carbohydrates:**

  Prioritize complex carbohydrates, essential for converting into glucose and providing energy. Opt for vegetables and certain fruits like oranges, tangerines, pears, grapefruits, apples, and kiwis during the evening to potentially aid in better sleep.

- **More Omega-3 Fatty Acids:**

  Integrate foods rich in omega-3 fatty acids, such as tuna, salmon, cold-water white fish, walnuts, Brazil nuts, and oils like olive and canola. Alternatively, consider an omega-3 fatty acid supplement.

As you navigate supporting your child's health with ADHD, it's crucial to be mindful of certain foods that might not provide the best nutrients for a healthy lifestyle. Here are some to consider avoiding:

- **Sugary Foods:**

  Sugar-rich foods not only add empty calories but can also contribute to health issues like type 2 diabetes, obesity, and heart disease. The Dietary Guidelines for Americans advise limiting sugars to less than 10% of daily caloric intake.

Examples of sugary foods to steer clear of include soda, concentrated fruit juices, candy, cake, cookies, and processed foods.

- **Simple Carbs:**

While not all simple carbohydrates are bad, many lack significant nutritional value and can lead to rapid spikes in blood sugar. Cut down on simple carbs like corn syrup, honey, sugar, white flour products, white rice, and potatoes without the skins.

- **Unhealthy Fats:**

While fat is necessary for vitamin absorption and cell growth, certain fats, like saturated fats, can pose health risks, such as elevated cholesterol levels. The American Heart Association recommends limiting saturated fats to 5%–6% of daily calorie intake. Foods high in saturated fat to avoid include those fried or baked in butter, ghee, lard, coconut oil, or palm oil, as well as high-fat dairy products and fatty meats.

- **Caffeine:**

If your child is on ADHD medication containing stimulants, adding caffeine might lead to excessive stimulation. While caffeine can provide a temporary focus boost, it cannot replace ADHD treatment. Monitor intake of coffee, tea, energy drinks, soda, and chocolate, especially if they seem to exacerbate anxiety, sleep disturbances, or stomach issues.

Now that you know the foods that are beneficial and harmful to your child, we need to correct some misconceptions many parents have when utilizing a diet for their ADHD child.

- **Myth 1: Eating sugary edibles and beverages triggers hyperactivity in kids with ADHD.**

Although numerous parents may attest that lots of sugar can lead to increased hyperactivity in their children, there is a lack of definitive proof establishing a direct link between sugar consumption and escalated hyperactivity in children with ADHD or without it. Eliminating sugar from the diet is not a cure for ADHD. However, it's crucial to acknowledge that an excess of sugar in the diet is unhealthy, and it is important to consume it moderately.

- **Myth 2: Adhering strictly to an elimination diet will significantly alleviate behavioral symptoms associated with ADHD.**

Although there is supporting evidence indicating that some children with ADHD might exhibit sensitivities to artificial food colors, flavorings, preservatives, salicylates, and other foods, there isn't a universally effective elimination diet for treating ADHD. Responses to eliminating specific foods or additives from the diet can vary, with some children showing positive outcomes while others exhibit no change.

- **Myth 3: High doses of vitamins and herbal supplements are advisable for children diagnosed with ADHD.**

There is insufficient evidence to support the efficacy and safety of high doses of vitamins, and in fact, such doses can pose harm to the body, particularly the liver. Similarly, research on herbal supplements for ADHD lacks robustness, making their effectiveness and safety uncertain. For most children, taking daily multivitamins is recommended. While supplementing with omega-3 fatty acids may hold potential benefits, further research is necessary to validate these claims. It is crucial to consult your child's physician before introducing any supplements.

A 7-day Meal Plan

To help you get started, I have created a week-long meal plan for your child with ADHD. Note that you are free to explore the other meals and be creative with the plan. This is just an example to guide you.

Monday:
Breakfast: Whole-wheat toast with scrambled eggs and spinach, berries with yogurt
Lunch: Chicken salad sandwich on whole-wheat bread with carrot sticks and hummus
Dinner: Salmon with roasted vegetables and brown rice
Snack: Handful of almonds and sliced apple
Tuesday:

Breakfast: Smoothie with spinach, banana, peanut butter, and milk
Lunch: Tuna salad in a whole-wheat pita with cucumber and tomato slices
Dinner: Turkey burgers on whole-wheat buns with sweet potato fries and green beans
Snack: Greek yogurt with granola and berries
Wednesday:
Breakfast: Oatmeal with chia seeds, nuts, and fruit
Lunch: Leftover turkey burger with quinoa salad
Dinner: Lentil soup with whole-wheat bread and side salad
Snack: Trail mix with nuts, seeds, and dried fruit
Thursday:
Breakfast: Whole-wheat pancakes with ricotta cheese and fruit

Lunch: Chicken and vegetable stir-fry with brown rice
Dinner: Baked tofu with roasted vegetables and quinoa
Snack: Cottage cheese with pineapple chunks
Friday:
Breakfast: Whole-wheat waffles with eggs and avocado
Lunch: Chicken quesadilla with black beans, cheese, and salsa on whole-wheat tortilla
Dinner: Pasta with tomato sauce, lean ground beef, and vegetables
Snack: Celery sticks with almond butter
Weekend:
Consider brunch: Combine breakfast and lunch for a relaxed, later meal.

Offer healthy options for outings: Pack fruits, vegetables, whole-wheat wraps, or homemade trail mix.

Get creative and involve your child: Allow them to choose healthy ingredients and help with simple tasks.

Understanding Food Sensitivities

Unlike allergies, food sensitivities don't prompt an immediate immune response. Instead, they lead to delayed and subtle reactions, giving rise to various symptoms like fatigue, headaches, mood swings, difficulty concentrating, hyperactivity, and impulsivity.

So, how do food sensitivities impact ADHD? While we don't fully understand the precise mechanisms, the following points suggest potential links:

Gut-Brain Connection:

> The gut microbiome plays a vital role in brain health and neurotransmitter production. Imbalances in gut bacteria associated with food sensitivities could influence attention and focus.

- **Inflammatory Response:** Certain food sensitivities may trigger low-grade inflammation, which can disrupt brain function and exacerbate ADHD symptoms.

- **Blood Sugar Fluctuations:**

  Foods high in sugar and refined carbohydrates can lead to blood sugar spikes and subsequent crashes, affecting energy levels and mood, which may intensify ADHD symptoms.

Guideline for Conducting an Elimination Diet

While exploring the potential connection between diet and ADHD, it's vital to know that elimination diets for children with ADHD are complex and require supervision by a qualified healthcare professional. Embarking on an elimination diet without professional guidance can pose risks and lead to nutritional deficiencies. Before starting, you need to:

- Seek guidance from a healthcare professional who can evaluate your child's unique needs, potential nutritional risks, and the suitability of an elimination diet for their specific situation.

- Explore potential contributors to your child's symptoms, such as medication side effects, sleep patterns, or underlying medical conditions.

- Understand that ongoing research on the diet-ADHD link indicates that individual responses to elimination diets vary greatly.

Below are some guidelines to help you consider eliminating diets for your child:

- **Gradual approach:**

    Begin by eliminating suspected trigger foods one at a time, focusing on common ones like dairy, gluten, sugar, and artificial additives.

- **Clear definition of triggers:**

    Determine the specific foods to eliminate based on available evidence, your child's preferences, and any suspected sensitivities.

- **Detailed food journal:**

    Keep a thorough record of all foods and beverages consumed, noting any observed changes in symptoms.

- **Nutritional adequacy:**

    Ensure your child receives all essential nutrients during the elimination phase by incorporating alternative food sources and considering supplements under professional guidance.

- **Reintroduction phase:**

    Slowly reintroduce eliminated foods one at a time, carefully monitoring reactions for at least 3-5 days.

- **Open communication:**

    Engage in your child in discussions about the process and decision-making, adapting communication to their age level.

Be prepared for potential difficulties and disruptions to meal routines, as eliminating diets can be challenging. Also, patience is key, because identifying sensitivities may take time. Stay committed to the plan and communicate any concerns to your healthcare professional.

Supplements and ADHD

Many parents turn to supplements to alleviate ADHD symptoms. Let's explore some common supplements and the research supporting their use. While studies often focus on children and teenagers due to the higher prevalence of ADHD in this age group, these supplements are generally considered safe for both adults and children.

- **Omega-3 and -6 Fatty Acids:**

    Omega-3 and -6 fatty acids, naturally occurring in foods like fish and flax seeds, are commonly taken as supplements, typically marketed as fish oil. Omega-3 and -6 supplements can improve various ADHD symptoms in children, including inattention, hyperactivity, reading abilities, and visual learning.

- **Iron:**

    Iron is involved in dopamine pathways in the brain, leading to the belief that low iron levels may exacerbate ADHD symptoms. Before considering iron supplements, it's advisable to consult with a healthcare provider to assess ferritin levels.

- **Magnesium L-Threonate:**

    Magnesium L-Threonate is a another form of magnesium, which could potentially improve symptoms. Research suggests that low magnesium levels might be linked to ADHD, and giving kids magnesium has shown promise in making their symptoms better. It can help with things like enhanced brain function, controlling impulses, mood regulation, and socializing. Adding magnesium to their routine might be a helpful way to support their overall well-being and manage ADHD symptoms effectively.

- **L-Theanine:**

    An amino acid found naturally in black and green tea. It is helpful to people with ADHD because it provides focus and energy without the jitters of pure caffeine. It has the ability improve on intrusive thoughts, concentration, anxiety, and can be used as an alternative to melatonin.

- **Probiotics:**

    Emerging research on the 'gut-brain axis' suggests a connection between gut bacteria and brain function. Some studies indicate that probiotics may reduce the risk of developing ADHD and can potentially alleviate symptoms and improve quality of life.

The Exercise-ADHD Connection

If your child grapples with the daily challenges of ADHD, physical activity is a powerful ally that many parents underestimate. Beyond its role in physical fitness, exercise can play a pivotal role in managing ADHD symptoms and unleashing your child's potential. Let's look at some of the of the benefits of exercise for your child's brain.

- **Boosts Brain Chemicals:**

    Engaging in physical activity increases the production of neurotransmitters like dopamine, norepinephrine, and serotonin, which are crucial for focus, attention, and mood regulation and are often deficient in ADHD.

- **Improves Executive Function:**

    Regular physical activity enhances skills such as planning, organization, and time management—all vital for children with ADHD.

- **Reduces Stress and Anxiety:**

    Exercise serves as a natural stress reliever, calming the mind and mitigating hyperactivity often associated with ADHD.

- **Increases Energy Levels:**

    Through promoting better sleep, physical activity contributes to improved energy levels and reduced fatigue – common challenges in ADHD.

- **Enhances Self-Esteem:**

    Participating in enjoyable physical activities and experiencing success can significantly boost your child's self-confidence and positive self-image.

While physical activities are important, consistency will make them more effective. If you find it challenging to create a consistent exercise routine for your child, the following tips will help you:

- ❖ **Find the Fun:** Identify activities your child enjoys, be they team sports, swimming, martial arts, dancing, or simply playing outside, as they are more likely to stick with what they find enjoyable.
- ❖ **Start Small and Gradually Increase:** Begin with brief sessions and progressively elevate the duration and intensity to prevent overwhelming your child.

- ❖ **Incorporate Short Bursts of Activity:** Break down longer exercises into shorter, engaging segments to maintain focus and energy.
- ❖ **Structure and Routine are Key:** Establish specific days and times for exercise, adhering to the schedule as consistently as possible.
- ❖ **Make it Social:** Encourage your child to partner up with friends or family members to add a fun, interactive element and increase motivation.
- ❖ **Positive Reinforcement:** Celebrate your child's achievements and emphasize the joy of movement rather than strict performance goals.
- ❖ **Be Patient and Flexible:** Know that it's not going to be a smooth ride. So, exercise patience, adjust the routine as needed, and focus on cultivating a positive experience with exercise for your child.

Mind-Body Practices

Apart from medication and therapy, mind-body practices offer an exciting avenue for addressing ADHD symptoms in children. These approaches leverage the profound connection between the mind and body, providing tools for self-regulation, focus improvement, and emotional well-being. Below are some benefits of mind-body practices for your child.

- ❖ **Improved Attention and Focus:**

    Activities like yoga and tai chi foster mindfulness and body awareness, enhancing the capacity to remain present and resist distractions.

- ❖ **Reduced Hyperactivity and Impulsivity:**

    The calming and grounding effects of these practices assist children in regulating their energy levels and controlling impulsive behaviors.

- ❖ **Enhanced Emotional Regulation:**

    Techniques such as deep breathing and meditation empower children with strategies to cope with stress, anxiety, and emotional fluctuations commonly associated with ADHD.

- ❖ **Increased Self-Awareness and Confidence:**

    Engaging in mind-body practices encourages introspection and self-understanding, thereby bolstering confidence and self-assurance in managing ADHD symptoms.

❖ **Fun and Engaging:**

Presenting these practices in a playful and enjoyable manner can appeal to children of various ages and interests. Here are some simple mind-body exercises you can try with your child to help them manage their ADHD:

❖ **5-Minute Breathing Break:**

Find a quiet spot where your child can sit comfortably. Encourage them to close their eyes and focus on their breathing. Inhale slowly through the nose, counting to four, hold for four counts, then exhale slowly through the mouth for eight counts. Repeat this process five times.

❖ **Mindful Movement:**

Play some calming music and invite your child to move their body freely. Encourage them to pay attention to how their body feels as they move and to focus on their breath.

- ❖ **Body Scan:**

    Help your child lie down in a comfortable position. Guide them to slowly scan their body from head to toe, noticing any areas of tension. Encourage them to relax each part of their body consciously.

- ❖ **Guided Visualization:**

    Take your child on a journey in their imagination to a peaceful place. Describe the scene in detail, including the sights, sounds, and smells. Encourage your child to immerse themselves fully in the experience.

Food and Mood

For years, we have heard the phrase, "You are what you eat," but let's delve deeper into why that matters. The concept of the gut-brain axis unveils a fascinating connection between our gut and brain, shedding light on how our diet can influence not just our physical health but also our mood, behavior, and mental health conditions like ADHD.

Think of the gut-brain axis as a two-lane highway. One lane carries signals from our gut to the brain, influenced by the trillions of bacteria residing in our gut microbiome. These bacteria produce various chemicals, including neurotransmitters like dopamine and serotonin, which play crucial roles in mood regulation, focus, and emotional stability.

The other lane carries signals from the brain to the gut, influenced by factors such as stress, emotions, and sleep patterns. These signals can impact the composition and function of gut bacteria, creating a feedback loop that can either amplify or alleviate certain ADHD symptoms. While research on the gut-brain axis and ADHD is still unfolding, some intriguing connections have emerged:

- **Gut microbiome imbalances:**

    Studies suggest that individuals with ADHD may have distinct gut bacterial compositions compared to those without ADHD. This imbalance could potentially contribute to inflammation, affect brain function, and exacerbate ADHD symptoms.

- **Food sensitivities:**

    Some children with ADHD might be sensitive to certain foods, leading to gut issues that could worsen ADHD symptoms.

- **Probiotics and prebiotics:**

    These live bacteria and their food sources have shown promise in certain studies for enhancing mood, focus, and attention in individuals with ADHD. However, further research is necessary to fully comprehend their effects.

    While researchers are still unraveling the exact mechanisms, there are several ways in which probiotics and gut health might affect mood and behavior in children:

- **Neurotransmitter Production:**

    The bacteria in the gut have the remarkable ability to produce neurotransmitters such as dopamine and serotonin, which play crucial roles in regulating mood, focus, and emotional well-being.

- **Inflammation Reduction:**

    Probiotics may contribute to reducing inflammation throughout the body. This reduction in inflammation can have a positive impact on mood and cognitive function, potentially leading to improvements in behavior.

- **Stress Management:**

Gut bacteria also play a role in influencing the body's stress response systems. By modulating these systems, probiotics may help improve emotional regulation and reduce anxiety in children.

Eating for Emotional Stability

In addressing emotional stability in children with ADHD, we cannot underestimate the role of nutrition. Here are some nutritional strategies that can support your child's emotional stability.

- **Focus on Whole, Unprocessed Foods:**

    Prioritize fruits, vegetables, whole grains, and lean proteins as they provide essential nutrients crucial for brain function, mood regulation, and sustained energy levels. You also have to limit processed foods, sugary drinks, and unhealthy fats, which can contribute to blood sugar fluctuations, inflammation, and difficulties in focus, potentially exacerbating emotional regulation challenges.

- **Promote Gut Health**

    Incorporate fermented foods like yogurt, kefir, and kimchi, as they contain beneficial bacteria (probiotics) that support gut health, potentially influencing mood and behaviors. Also, ensure adequate fiber intake from fruits, vegetables, and whole grains to nourish gut bacteria and maintain a healthy gut microbiome.

- **Balance Blood Sugar:**

Choose low-glycemic index (GI) carbohydrates like whole grains, beans, and certain fruits to regulate glucose release into the bloodstream, preventing energy levels and mood fluctuations. You also need to limit the consumption of sugary drinks and refined carbohydrates, which can lead to rapid blood sugar spikes followed by crashes, resulting in irritability and difficulty managing emotions. Instead, incorporate healthy fats like avocado, nuts, and seeds, which promote satiety and help stabilize blood sugar levels.

In conclusion, understanding the impact of nutrition and exercise on the ADHD brain unveils powerful tools for supporting your child's well-being. While not a magical cure, a tailored ADHD diet, rich in proteins, complex carbohydrates, and omega-3 fatty acids, can potentially enhance focus and manage symptoms. Also, embracing exercise and incorporating consistent physical activity can significantly benefit the attention, executive function, and emotional well-being of your child. Aside from nutrition and exercise, other allies can support your child. In the next chapter, we will explore these allies and how they benefit your child.

Key Takeaways

- Nutrition and exercise as potent tools for managing ADHD symptoms.

- Craft an individualized ADHD diet, emphasizing high-protein, complex carbohydrates, and omega-3 fatty acids while avoiding sugary, simple carb-rich, and unhealthy fat-laden foods.

- Embrace mind-body exercises like breathing breaks, mindful movement, body scans, and guided visualizations to improve attention, reduce hyperactivity, and enhance emotional regulation.

- Consider omega-3 fatty acids, iron, magnesium, melatonin, and probiotics as supplements, but consult a healthcare professional for personalized advice.

- Prioritize whole, unprocessed foods, promote gut health with fermented foods, and balance blood sugar levels to support emotional stability in children with ADHD.

Chapter Nine

Allies in Action - Advocating for ADHD in Education and Beyond

"We are stronger when we stand together."

- Jean Grey (X-men)

Many parents often think they have to bear the burden of their child with ADHD alone. But the truth is that there are allies you can work with to help you manage ADHD in your child. One of those allies is an educator and that's because the school system is a major part of your child's daily life. Here's why the educational system plays a crucial role in your child's life.

- **Early Identification and Intervention:**

    Schools are often the first to notice ADHD symptoms, allowing for early diagnosis and intervention, which can greatly influence your child's long-term development.

- **Tailored Learning:**

    ADHD can impact attention and focus, making traditional classrooms challenging. The educational system must adapt teaching methods to accommodate individual learning styles and address the specific needs of students with ADHD.

- **Social and Emotional Support:**

    Children with ADHD may encounter social and emotional hurdles. Schools can create a supportive environment that fosters positive interactions, self-esteem, and emotional well-being.

- **Collaboration and Communication:**

    Effective support requires collaboration between parents, teachers, and professionals. The educational system should encourage open communication to ensure a holistic approach to helping students with ADHD thrive.

Sometimes, navigating the educational system for a child with ADHD can feel overwhelming, but you don't have to give up or think you will not explore that ally. You only need to take the right steps to help your child. However, further research is necessary to fully comprehend their effects.

- **Seek Diagnosis and Evaluation:**

Start by getting a comprehensive evaluation from a qualified professional to confirm the ADHD diagnosis and understand your child's strengths and weaknesses.

- **Develop an Individualized Education Plan (IEP) or 504 Plan:**

These plans outline specific accommodations and modifications to support your child's learning needs. Collaborate with the school to develop a customized plan for your child.

- **Advocate for Your Child:**

To ensure the effective implementation of the plan, understand your child's rights and collaborate with teachers and administrators. Be prepared to advocate for any necessary adjustments.

- **Build a Support Network:**

  Connect with other parents, educators, and professionals who can offer guidance and support throughout your child's educational journey.

Understanding your Child's Rights

Many parents struggle to work with educators to provide their children with the necessary support because they are unaware of their rights. Here are some benefits that your child can receive:

- **Individuals with Disabilities Education Act (IDEA):**

  Ensures that students with disabilities, including ADHD, receive a free and appropriate public education.

- **Section 504 of the Rehabilitation Act:**

  It prohibits discrimination in federally funded programs, including schools, and provides accommodations for students with disabilities.

❖ **National Resource Center on ADHD:**

Offers valuable information and resources for parents, educators, and professionals.

❖ **CHADD (Children and Adults with Attention-Deficit/Hyperactivity Disorder):**

An advocacy organization providing support, resources, and information for individuals and families affected by ADHD.

Strategies for Effective Advocacy

Now that you know your rights and the resources available for your child, there is a way to go about advocating for your child. Remember that your goal is to provide the necessary support for your child. Therefore, you need to be strategic to ensure effectiveness. Let's dive in.

● **Knowledge is Power:**

We cannot overemphasize the importance of education when advocating for your child. Utilize resources like CHADD, the National Resource Center on ADHD, to understand ADHD and relevant educational laws. You also need to understand your child's unique needs. Observe and document your child's strengths, challenges, and learning style for effective advocacy.

- **Communication is Key:**

  Just like in any relationship, open communication is crucial. Establish positive relationships with teachers by communicating your child's needs respectfully and clearly. You also need to involve your child in advocacy, encouraging them to share their experiences with teachers. It's best to maintain detailed records of interactions. That way, you can track your child's progress.

- **Take Action:**

Discuss your child's needs and explore classroom accommodations with your child's teacher. You can also request an IEP or 504 plan if needed and advocate for a formal plan outlining specific modification.

- **Be Persistent and Proactive:**

You must always seek clarification and advocate repeatedly for evolving needs. You can also join other parent and advocacy groups to share experiences and strategies.

Equipping Your Child with ADHD For the Workforce

As your child begins to grow, they will find themselves in environments different from home. They will grow to become adults, and they need to know how to function optimally in the workforce. Here are ways you can equip your child with helpful skills that will help them navigate their way in the work environment.

- **Develop Self-Advocacy Skills:**

    Teach your child to express their strengths, weaknesses, and needs effectively in various situations.

- **Time Management and Organization:**

    Assist your child in developing strategies for time management, task planning, and staying organized.

- **Social and Emotional Skills:**

    Foster social skills such as communication and collaboration. Encourage emotional regulation techniques to manage stress.

- **Explore Career Options:**

    Discuss career paths aligned with your child's interests, skills, and learning style. Explore the accommodations and support available in different workplaces.

- **Practice Job Interview Skills:**

    Role-play job interview scenarios, helping your child develop confident and articulate responses.

Creating ADHD-Friendly Workplaces

The responsibility of creating an ADHD-friendly environment majorly depends on the employer. Below are ways employers can make their workplace suitable for someone with ADHD:

- **Open Communication:** Organizations need to encourage open discussions about ADHD in the workplace. Provide information and training to colleagues and managers.

- **Flexible Work Arrangements:**

    They should offer flexibility with remote work options, flexible hours, or breaks as needed.

- **Assistive Technology:**

    Companies must provide access to assistive technologies aiding in organization, time management, and focus.

- **Minimize Distractions:**

    They must create a work environment with minimal distractions and noise.

- **Mentorship and Support:**

    They can implement mentorship and support programs to help employees with ADHD navigate the workplace and thrive in their roles.

Career Planning

As we have explored how to make your child perform optimally in a work environment, you also need to be involved when choosing their career. Without mincing words, navigating career planning for a child with ADHD will be challenging, but fear not! Let's explore how to recognize exciting career possibilities perfectly tailored to your child.

- **Let's Talk About Your Child:**

    First things first, let's dive into what makes your child tick. What are their passions and interests? Think about the activities that make them lose track of time. What comes naturally to them, and what do others commend them for? Also, what hurdles do they face? Pinpoint specific tasks or environments that pose difficulties. And when envisioning their ideal work setting, do they thrive in a fast-paced, collaborative atmosphere, or do they prefer a more structured, independent approach?

- **Explore their Strengths:**

As previously said, many ADHD traits are like hidden superpowers, even in the workplace. Think about your child's ability to hyper-focus on tasks they enjoy, their knack for creative problem-solving, and their boundless energy and enthusiasm for projects they are passionate about.

- **Consider their Challenges:**

    Let's acknowledge areas where your child might need a little extra support or accommodations at work. Whether it's flexible work arrangements, noise-canceling headphones, or assistive technology, these are tools to help them thrive, not limitations.

- **Discover Potential Career Paths:**

Based on their interests, strengths, and challenges, you can explore some broad career categories. From creative fields like design and writing to entrepreneurship, technology, helping professions, science and research, and sales and marketing, there's a wide array of paths to consider.

Building a Supportive Community

Living with ADHD presents challenges, but finding support can greatly ease the journey for your child. You can either find a support group, build one, or leverage available community resources. Let's dive in.

- Finding Support Group

❖ **Online Communities:**

   Explore virtual connections and support through platforms like CHADD or online forums.

❖ **Local Organizations**:

Look into mental health organizations or community centers for in-person support groups.

- ❖ **Demographic-Specific Groups**:

    Seek out groups tailored to adults with ADHD, parents of children with ADHD, or specific age or gender demographics.

- ❖ **Professional Organizations**:

    Consider groups led by therapists or educators specializing in ADHD for professional guidance.

● Creating Your Support Group:

❖ **Identify Needs**: Determine what specific gap your group will fill and how it will operate.

❖ **Spread the Word**: Use various channels to attract potential members, such as social media, community boards, or personal networks.

❖ **Set Ground Rules:** Establish guidelines for respectful communication and confidentiality.

❖ **Facilitate Interaction:** Encourage sharing experiences and peer support within the group.

- ❖ **Consider Professional Guidance:** Consulting with experienced facilitators can provide valuable support.

● Leveraging Community Resources:

- ❖ **Mental Health Professionals:** Seek therapy or group sessions with professionals specializing in ADHD.

- ❖ **Educational Resources:** Take advantage of workshops and resources offered by schools or libraries.

- ❖ **Disability Rights Organizations:** Explore the advocacy and support provided by these groups.

- ❖ **Financial Assistance Programs:** Look into aids for therapy, medication, or assistive technology.

- ❖ **Career Counseling Services**: Find guidance on navigating the workforce with ADHD.

In conclusion, parents often feel alone in managing their child's ADHD, but there are allies, particularly within the educational system. The school plays a crucial role in early identification, tailored learning, and providing social and emotional support. Aside from the educational sector, building a supportive community is equally important. Support groups, whether found online, locally, or created, along with leveraging community resources, contribute significantly to easing the journey of your child.

As we proceed to the next chapter, we will explore the life skills needed for them to navigate this dynamic world.

Key Takeaways

- Schools are key allies in identifying ADHD symptoms early, tailoring learning experiences, and providing crucial social and emotional support for children with ADHD.

- Effective support for children with ADHD requires collaboration and open communication between parents, teachers, and professionals to ensure a holistic approach to education.

- Understanding laws like IDEA and Section 504 empowers you to advocate for your child's rights to receive appropriate education and accommodations.

- Successful advocacy involves strategic steps such as seeking a diagnosis, developing individualized plans, maintaining detailed records, and persistently advocating for necessary accommodations.

- Employers can contribute to creating ADHD-friendly workplaces by fostering open communication, offering flexible work arrangements, providing assistive technology, minimizing distractions, and offering mentorship.

Chapter Ten

The Symphony of Support - Building a community

"We have a saying, my people. Don't kill if you can wound, don't wound if you can subdue, don't subdue if you can pacify, and don't raise your hand at all until you've first extended it."

-Superman

It is a common belief that it takes a whole village to raise a child. It does! It is not a one-person thing. As a parent, you don't want to underestimate the power of kind words or actions such as, "Can I drop that off for you on my way home?" or, "Can you help me pick up my child on your way home?" The truth is, no matter how you've prepared to raise a child, you still need the right networking to effectively raise a child with ADHD, just like other parents do. It would help if you had shoulders to lean on and people to rub minds together. It would help if you also had people who have been there to share experiences and personal struggles with you and find inner peace that will keep you going despite the hurdles.

A formidable local support system plays a significant role in your child's mental and physical health as they grow, and as a parent of children with ADHD, you must ensure you build strong support where you and your child can receive ample support from different people in your immediate environment.

The Value of a Strong Support Network

In the course of raising a child struggling with ADHD, you will certainly encounter moments where you need the support of others. During these times, you need to rely on some people around you to navigate difficult situations, or you may even be overwhelmed and about to give up. The power of a formidable community is so profound and can significantly impact and make the whole process easy for you. Every act of support, whether in a word of encouragement or providing support in raising your child, leaves a lasting impression on your life and that of the child.

As a parent of a child with ADHD, it is a common thing to face that proverbial rough patch in the road of parenting that makes one feel lost, unable to control anything, and overwhelmed; the support system you create becomes crucial. The people in your village cycle remind you of your strength, encourage you when you like giving up, and give you all the unwavering belief that you need to overcome any challenge along the way.

Creating Your Village

If you have not found any local system that understands your child or family's needs, or you think you deserve something better, you can decide to create your own village for parents like you who want their children to thrive but are not sure how to get people's help in achieving it. There is no need to wander lost and alone. If you discover you don't get as much help as you want in a place or there is none at all, it is a wise step if you can create one where incredible give-and-take can happen.

The Benefits of a Supportive Community

There is nothing better than seeking advice from people who have done something before. It saves you from stress and helps you avoid many mistakes. As a parent of a child with ADHD, you must know that to do incredible things in raising your child, you need incredible people. Even though you know a few things about raising a child, you can and should tap into supportive communities to draw support along the way.

When you need a recommendation for a good lawyer, a gift idea, or a doctor, what do you do? You can either ask people you know and trust or search online and read a few online reviews about their services. Resources and information flow from and through networks.

More so, one of the essential things about having a supportive community is that it gives you a sense of purpose and belonging. Besides being a parent, togetherness is so central to our lives as people or human beings. We are social beings who are wired to rely on social connections and networks. Finding other people with the same value helps us see that we are not alone. We gain influence and have access to share information.

More so, having a strong local community around you provides not only physical support but also emotional support. Being a member of a community helps handle loneliness. Most people who slide into depression are often disassociated from people. The value of a local community is even more essential nowadays when many people get isolated due to economic struggle.

How to Build and Maintain a Support Network

Everyone needs a support network that they can rely on at any time for encouragement and support. However, getting one that matches one's desires and wants may be difficult at times. If you love the idea of becoming a member or having a support network where your desires are captured but are wondering how you can get started, below are a few ways to achieve this;

Set clear goals - The first step is to know who the potential members of the community are. Who is the community for, and why did that exist? Regardless, having a north star can give you a direction and what you are expecting from each member.

Engage members - look for parents of children with ADHD whom you would love to come together with to foster relationships, share similar experiences, recount struggles, and propose ways to solve any parenting issue. Tell friends, family members, and other people about it to attract people of similar interest.

Set the Structure - After you've got people who are interested in becoming members, you put in the structure of leadership and outline programs and meeting times and dates when you will come together (physically or virtually) to discuss your experience and share possible ways out. This will help each member understand their roles and become accountable.

The Role of Family, Friends, Professionals, and Online and Local Support Groups

Whether you are building or maintaining a community network, you must remember the incredible contributions of people in your closest circle. You should know that you need your friends and family to be your pillar of support, especially at the moment when you are about to give up on your child's inabilities. Having a strong support network of family and friends can help enhance your mental and emotional abilities to be strong enough for your child. These people include your loved ones, friends, and family. It can be devastating when the people you need to help you are not where to be found.

Also, experts play a significant role in helping you through difficult times. Experts receive professional training to provide guidance and advice on raising your child. They have a wealth of experience in cases like yours and can tell you how best to handle them. So, as you are thinking of building a community of friends and family to provide strong support, you should pay attention to the role of an expert.

An expert diagnosis and recommends a support system during a difficult time. An expert reserves an unbiased confidant who listens without judgment. Having an expert in your life as a parent of a child can be transformative when facing challenges, especially when you are finding it hard to cope with your child. That kind of empathetic presence can offer hope when all is lost.

More so, social media and online groups offer incredible support, give you access to a network, and help you connect with others who share your interests. So, it would help if you looked for groups whose mission and vision aligned with yours and joined the community so you could easily share your own experiences and challenges. However, remember that being active on the platforms matters. The more active you are in the group you join, the more likely you are to make meaningful engagements.

Engaging with Educators and Professionals

Raising a child is not a one-person show; it requires the efforts of many people, especially when it involves a child with special needs. In cases like this, parents don't rely on the effort alone. Even though they play a key role in raising their child, they need the support of people outside their vicinity.

Children with ADHD go to school even if learning some subjects might require a lot of effort. So, parents should know how they can liaise with school authorities and educators on how to create an inclusive educational system to accommodate children with special needs. Teachers need to understand why they need to put in extra academic efforts to ensure that no child, regardless of their challenge, is left behind. This starts with teachers knowing their students, what their needs are, and creating examples that match their interests.

However, as a parent, you must understand the value of partnership. You should partner with your child's school authority to create community building in the classroom. How schools and parents communicate together goes a long way toward determining how formidable the support network will be.

Advocating for your child's needs

Being an advocate means speaking on behalf of your child. There is no doubt that your child has needs, and you are the only person who can dutifully have a voice. You are in the best position to ask questions, raise concerns, and ask for help when needed. Advocating for your child also includes teaching your child how and why they should speak up. But, you know, it is quite a daunting task to do.

Some parents found it uncontrollable or difficult to speak to educators about their child's needs. Most of them think it's their place. Or perhaps they always remember the ugly incident they had when they did. And in fact, some people don't even know what to say, how to say it, or when to have it said.

However, as a parent, you should know that when things are not going well in school, you are supposed to speak up—be a voice for them. And it would help if you did not wait until the next teacher-parent conference. You know your child's strengths, weaknesses, and interests, and you should always be ready to voice them out whenever there is a need for that. Doing this helps to ensure your child has the support they need to thrive.

Collaborative problem-solving

Are you tired of yelling, shouting, nagging, and constant power struggles between you and your child? If the behavioral chart you drew is not helping matters and both rewards and punishments have failed, the next turn to take is collaborative problem-solving, popularly known as CPS.

Studies have affirmed that traditional discipline doesn't work because it doesn't result in improved relationships or behavior between parents and their children. Experts deem the CPS effective as a relational discipline that reduces the stress parents endure while instilling positive and correct behavioral patterns in their children.

As a parent of a child with ADHD, it is crucial to know how this approach can be helpful. It teaches you how to work collaboratively with your child with ADHD to improve their behavior instead of waiting for them to do it themselves. What makes this approach unique is that it immerses you in the system. You are part of the process of a child's behavioral formation. In doing this, the approach helps you reduce undesirable outcomes and helps you focus on what matters. It teaches you to figure out a potential issue and deploy strategies to address it instead of waiting for your child to do so alone. In this case, you are not only teaching your child how to develop certain behaviors, but you are also teaching yourself how to adapt to difficult situations together. Over time, studies have affirmed that the approach helps reduce behavioral expectations that often lead to frustration and emotional outbursts from most parents.

Inclusivity and Advocacy

It is a known fact that teachers and school management play a significant role in identifying, managing, and referring to children with ADHD. Teachers are the most important, followed by family. This is why teachers, parents, and school authorities need to come together to build an inclusive educational curriculum that will capture not only the learning disabilities of children with ADHD but also their interests.

In most of our schools, children with ADHD often lack focus and exhibit a high frequency of disruptive behaviors. So, there is a need for strategies, such as family school success, to help these children navigate through the different challenges they face with their academics at school.

Also, it captures how parents can be of help too. This strategy teaches parents how to assist their children with studying at home. On this, the strategy focuses on goal-setting and parent tutoring. An initial step is to break down the children's homework assignment into smaller, more manageable subunits. By breaking down homework assignments into smaller, more manageable subunits, children can feel less overwhelmed, record their progress, and receive necessary positive reinforcement.

Additionally, the inclusivity system can encourage parents to help their children develop study skills through parent tutoring sessions designed to help students learn materials and get ready for examinations and tests.

When it comes to policy changes, you must become familiar with personalized education plans to advocate for a child effectively. Or, better yet, advocate for it. This system helps take into account a child's specific needs and outlines a modified curriculum with practical goals for academic excellence. Educators, teachers, parents, and other experts should actively engage in the development of a personalized education plan to drive inclusivity. They should also monitor the child's progress on the individualized education plan carefully to know if they are meeting the standard educational requirements and goals and make some adjustments where necessary.

Sharing your journey to inspire others

We know that sharing our journeys can be a very effective way to inspire others and bring back their hope, but it is always easy to get started. That's why, if you ask other parents who have successfully raised a child with ADHD to the point that they have explored their potential, when they tell you about how many times, they fail and the kind of challenges they face, you will feel like you can't give the same effort. But in an actual sense, those stories are not meant to weigh you down. So, it is important that when someone is sharing their stories with you, you focus on the fact that they overcame. That's where the motivation is.

You see, when there is no pain, there can't be gain. And as a parent who wants their children to thrive, regardless of their difficulties, you don't focus on the pain but on the gain that will come after that. Experiences, bad or good, are meant to shape our lives. Some bad ones are better than we portray them to be. They only require some extra effort to push through.

Therefore, always be willing to share your experience, particularly when you are with parents whose children are struggling with special abilities. It gives them hope that they can overcome several challenges that come with parenting children with special needs. However, when you are doing this, you must state some practical steps that helped you succeed. Also, it would help if you did not forget to add when and how you did it. There are stages to learning how to cope with children with special needs, and it would be good if you could share with them not only the challenges but also tips that helped you overcome each challenge at each stage along the way.

The Impact of Community on a Child's Success

As you have learned, different factors and people's contributions are significant for any child struggling with ADHD to succeed. It is a common thing for parents to show love and care for their children with ADHD. Teachers also make meaningful contributions to instill academic and moral skills. But one other factor whose contribution to the success of any child is huge is society.

Society influences the behavior and actions of children with ADHD just like it does for others. It regulates their actions and behaviors by teaching social cues that help enhance their communication with people around them. It does this by helping them develop some social skills that are necessary for engaging in effective communication. These skills are useful in regulating their emotions and engaging in effective interactions with their peers. When children engage in active communication, they learn how to cooperate, negotiate, and solve problems with others. With these abilities, they are also able to build positive relationships with people around them.

In conclusion, having a strong support system can enhance overall child development and offer you the safe landing you want when things are getting harder, and you already feel like you are losing out. Along with supporting your mental health and reducing stress and anxiety, having a support system improves your capacity to network with people with common interests. Raising a child with special needs is not something you should do alone. Many people have successfully raised their children with ADHD, and you can learn from them. Also, some experts have a wealth of experience and are willing to guide you through using provable tips. What you are left to do is take the bold step of finding them, networking with them, whether physically or virtual People believe that when you share a problem, it becomes half-solved. a shared problem is half-solved. When you share your challenges, these people can offer advice and encourage you to keep pushing. After all, it is always good to have shoulders to cry on when things get harder.

Key Takeaways

- A child is not only the product of their parents but of an entire society. It takes two to give birth to a child, but a whole community to raise the child.

- As a parent of a child with ADHD, society is your pillar of support. Having the right network is important in effectively raising your child to maximize their full potential.
- Advocating for your child includes training them to be able to speak for themselves and also do the same for them, especially in schools.
- Also, partnering with teachers and your child's school authority is the best way to advocate and build an inclusive educational system that supports your child's needs and interests.

Conclusion

This isn't just the closing chapter of a book; it's the beginning of a movement. We have embarked on a transformative journey, not only to empower children with ADHD but to redefine the narrative surrounding their unique neurodiversity. While we celebrate the end of this book, let's remember that the story is far from complete.

We need to celebrate children with ADHD as much as we can. Do you know why? Children with ADHD aren't confined by their challenges; they exemplify resilience and surmount obstacles. They embody boundless creativity; their minds are filled with fresh perspectives and groundbreaking ideas. Let's honor their strengths, not merely manage their differences.

It's time to redefine the discourse. ADHD isn't a deficiency; it's a divergent mode of thinking that enriches the world with a distinctive and invaluable viewpoint. This is a call. Be an advocate and encourage your child to be a champion and a superhero for yourself and others. Let them share their narratives, raise awareness, and dismantle the stigma. Together, let's construct a world where every child with ADHD can unleash their inner superhero and soar

Reflecting on the Journey

As we turn the final page, let's pause to reflect on our journey and the transformation we have undergone. Our quest wasn't merely to "raise superheroes" with ADHD but to rewrite the narrative surrounding this exceptional neurodiversity.

Undoubtedly, this path was filled with challenges. You, the parent, have confronted countless obstacles, struggled with mixed emotions, and poured your love and support into your child. Do you know that you also deserve an award? If not for anything, for raising a superhero. You are a superhero in your own right.

Together, we have shattered myths and misconceptions. We have underscored the importance of early intervention, effective strategies, and transparent communication. Above all, we've instilled in our children a sense of empowerment and pride.

As you journey ahead, here are some toolkits you must always harness.

- **Embrace:**

    Embrace and celebrate your child's unique neurodiversity.

- **Collaborate:**

    Forge alliances with educators, professionals, and fellow parents to cultivate supportive environments.

- **Communicate:**

    Foster an open and honest dialogue to understand and support your child effectively.

- **Empower:**

    Arm your child with the tools and strategies they need to thrive.

- **Advocate:**

    Be a vocal advocate for your child, champion their rights, and strive for a world that embraces inclusivity.

Empowerment in Action

These strategies above are not just abstract ideas; they are blueprints for real-life triumphs. Picture a young artist with ADHD channeling hyper-focus into complex designs and award-winning, gallery-worthy pieces, inspiring others with their distinctive vision.

Imagine a young entrepreneur with ADHD, where creative thinking births innovative solutions, hyper-focus conquers challenges, and social skills attract investors. See them launch prosperous businesses and create jobs, proving ADHD does not impede entrepreneurial success.

Imagine a future scientist with ADHD: their curiosity fueled ground-breaking research and unconventional thinking, leading to discoveries. Picture them making life-changing contributions, winning awards, and showcasing that ADHD can spur scientific breakthroughs.

See an athlete with ADHD converting high energy into exceptional stamina, adaptability giving an edge in fast-paced sports, and determination driving peak performance. Witness them breaking records and competing at elite levels.

These glimpses reveal the boundless potential within children with ADHD. By empowering them with the right tools and nurturing them in a supportive environment, they can transform their unique strengths into superpowers, achieving success in any field they choose.

The Community's Role

It's often said that no man can thrive in isolation. In the journey of empowering children with ADHD, know that you are not alone but part of a collective effort, each contributing to creating a world where they can thrive.

As a parent or guardian, you are to create a nurturing environment by understanding your child's strengths, implementing effective strategies, and advocating for their needs. Share your experiences, connect with others, and be a pillar of strength for your child and the community.

Educators also have a role in creating classrooms where every child feels valued by embracing neurodiversity, tailoring learning experiences, and fostering understanding among peers. They can advocate for accommodations, collaborate with parents, and champion inclusive education.

A professional can equip children with ADHD with tools for success through diagnosis, therapy, and support services. They can stay informed, collaborate, and advocate for evidence-based practices that empower individuals with ADHD.

Even society plays its part. They are involved in dispelling myths, challenging stigma, and promoting acceptance to create a society that embraces neurodiversity.

We can envision schools where every child feels empowered, workplaces that celebrate diversity, and communities that embrace individual differences when everyone in the community plays their role.

Long-life Learning and Adaptation

As your child grows and changes, so do the challenges and opportunities they face. You need to embrace the evolving nature of parenting, which requires ongoing learning and adaptation.

View it as a journey where your child's changing needs demand different tools for support. Don't hesitate to seek new knowledge, explore diverse strategies, and adapt your approach. Remember, there's no one-size-fits-all solution, and what works today might not work tomorrow.

Embrace the learning process by staying informed through books, articles, and expert research on ADHD. Connect with your fellow parents for shared experiences and mutual learning. Seek guidance from professionals like therapists, educators, and coaches tailored to offer support.

Every step in your learning journey empowers your child to take theirs. By continuously seeking knowledge and adapting your approach, you not only support their growth but also model invaluable lifelong learning skills.

You can explore these resources to further your journey:

- CHADD Website: https://www.chadd.org/
- NIMH ADHD Information: https://www.nimh.nih.gov/health/topics/attention-deficit-hyperactivity-disorder-adhd
- https://www.understood.org/

The Legacy of Change

Now that you have been armed with a wealth of understanding and strategies, it's best that you don't keep it to yourself. Share your insights with others—parents, educators, friends, and family. By debunking myths and sharing your experiences, you become a guiding light, illuminating the path for future generations.

This world is within reach, and you hold the key. By advocating for change, promoting inclusion, and challenging harmful stereotypes, you pave the way for a brighter future for children with ADHD.

Reflect on your journey from debunking myths about "fidgety kids" to embracing the complexities of neurodiversity. This mirrors a cultural shift happening right now. We are progressing towards a world that acknowledges and embraces individual differences, not just in theory but in practice.

The Final Message

Before you leave, pause for a moment. You have embarked on an extraordinary journey, navigating through challenges, celebrating triumphs, and uncovering the potential within your child. Know that you are not walking this path alone.

This community, this movement, stands shoulder to shoulder with you, offering support and encouragement every step of the way.

Remember, ADHD is not a burden. It's a latent superpower awaiting its moment to shine. With the right tools, support, and belief, your child can overcome any obstacle and achieve greatness. Now, it's time for action. This book is more than just a manual; it's a roadmap. Carry its message forward and share it with others. Advocate for understanding, challenge misconceptions, and champion neurodiversity in all its forms.

Speak up for those whose voices go unheard. Bridge the gaps between communities.

Together, let's forge a world where every child with ADHD feels empowered, supported, and celebrated. Let's rewrite the prevailing narrative, dismantle the stigma, and unleash the hidden superheroes residing within each one of them.

To my beloved Family,

From the depths of my heart, I extend my sincerest gratitude to each one of you for the unwavering strength, patience, support, and love you've shown me through our many travels around the world. Our journey together, marked by obstacles and challenges, has been the foundation upon which I've built my dreams. Your steadfast belief in my abilities, even when faced with adversity, has been the cornerstone of my journey to write a book that aspires to touch and improve lives. In moments of doubt, it was your conviction that rekindled my resolve and inspired me to press forward. Your encouragement has been my guiding light, illuminating the path when the road seemed daunting and the nights endless. Without you, this dream would not have been possible. I love you to infinity.

I am profoundly thankful to the Heavenly Father for His countless blessings. It is through His grace that I have been molded into the person I am today, equipped with the determination and spirit to embark on this meaningful endeavor. The journey of writing this book has been more than a pursuit of a personal dream; it has been a testament to the power of faith, the beauty of shared hopes, and the strength derived from a family's love.

To say 'thank you' feels inadequate to express the depth of my gratitude. Yet, these words carry the weight of my appreciation and recognition of your invaluable contribution to my life and this project. I am immensely grateful for your sacrifices, your unwavering support, and the endless love you've bestowed upon me. Together, we have sown the seeds for a legacy that, God willing, will flourish and extend its reach far beyond our imaginations.

With all my love and deepest thanks,

Phoenix J. Waldren

The Super Signal in the Sky

Wowzers! You've soared through the pages and now you're ready to spread the super news. You have the know-how to help super kids with ADHD zoom to their potential, and guess what? Your mission isn't over yet! By sharing your super thoughts about this book on Amazon, you're lighting up the sky for other super parents. Your review is like the beam that guides them to the super secrets they're searching for. It's like passing the baton in the biggest relay race ever! And you're not just a runner; you're a super coach, and supporter, So, if you could take a flash of a moment to leave your honest review, you'll be the spark that helps another family light up their world. It's more than just words; it's passing the torch of super knowledge. A mega thank you for joining the super parent team. Remember, every super kid with ADHD shines bright because of the super support they have – and you are part of that brilliance.

\>> Zoom over here to leave your super review on Amazon.

References

ADDitude Magazine. (n.d.). 10 Tips for Teachers with ADHD Students. https://www.additudemag.com/teaching-tips-for-adhd-students/

ADDitude Magazine. (n.d.). Building Self-Esteem in Children with ADHD. https://www.additudemag.com/adhd-in-kids-building-self-esteem/

ADDitude Magazine. (n.d.). Teaching Self-Control: Evidence-Based Tips. https://www.additudemag.com/teaching-self-control-evidence-based-tips/

ADDitude. (n.d.). How to Help Children with ADHD Focus. https://www.additudemag.com/focus-techniques-for-adhd-kids/

ADDitude. (n.d.). How to Help Kids Understand Their ADHD. https://www.additudemag.com/understand-adhd-in-kids/

ADDitude. (n.d.). The Right Foods for Managing ADHD Symptoms. https://www.additudemag.com/adhd-diet-nutrition-foods-to-eat

ADHD Advocacy Canada. (n.d.). Advocating for Your Child in School. https://adhdsupportcanada.com/advocating-for-your-child-in-school/

Attention Deficit Disorder Association (ADDA). (n.d.). Navigating the Workplace. https://add.org/navigating-the-workplace/

Bailey, E. (n.d.). ADHD and School: Tips for Teachers to Help Students Succeed. Very well Mind. https://www.verywellmind.com/adhd-and-school-tips-for-teachers-20481

Breggin, P. (2017, November). The Myth of ADHD: 10 Reasons to Stop Drugging Kids for Acting Like Kids. Psychology Today.

https://www.psychologytoday.com/us/blog/psychiatry-through-the-looking-glass/201711/the-myth-adhd-10-reasons-stop-drugging-kids-acting-kids

CHADD. (n.d.). Emotional Regulation and ADHD. https://chadd.org/adhd-weekly/emotional-regulation-and-adhd/

CHADD. (n.d.). Helping Kids with ADHD Resolve Conflicts. https://chadd.org/adhd-weekly/helping-kids-with-adhd-resolve-conflicts/

Cherry, K. (n.d.). ADHD in the Classroom: Effective Strategies for Teachers. Verywell Mind. https://www.verywellmind.com/adhd-in-the-classroom-2794845

Cherry, K. (n.d.). The Benefits of ADHD: The Surprising Advantages of Attention Deficit Hyperactivity Disorder. Verywell Mind. https://www.verywellmind.com/benefits-of-adhd-4117740

Child Mind Institute. (n.d.). 10 Tips for Helping Kids with ADHD Succeed. https://childmind.org/article/10-tips-for-helping-kids-with-adhd-succeed/

Child Mind Institute. (n.d.). 7 Ways to Boost Self-Esteem and Confidence in Children with ADHD. https://childmind.org/article/7-ways-to-boost-self-esteem-and-confidence-in-children-with-adhd/

Child Mind Institute. (n.d.). School Accommodations for ADHD: Teacher Tips. https://childmind.org/article/school-accommodations-for-adhd-teacher-tips/

Child Mind Institute. (n.d.). Setting Up a Routine for an ADHD Child. https://childmind.org/article/setting-up-a-routine-for-your-adhd-child/

Child Mind Institute. (n.d.). The Power of Support Groups for ADHD. https://childmind.org/article/the-power-of-support-groups-for-adhd/

EdTech Magazine. (n.d.). How Adaptive Learning Technology Can Help Students Succeed. https://edtechmagazine.com/k12/article/2021/01/how-adaptive-learning-technology-can-help-students-succeed

Healthline. (n.d.). The Best ADHD Diet: What to Eat (and avoid) for Kids and Adults. https://www.healthline.com/health/adhd/best-diet

Morin, A. (n.d.). How to Encourage a Positive Self-Image in Kids with ADHD Understood. https://www.understood.org/articles/en/encouraging-positive-self-image-in-kids-with-adhd

The Understood Team. (n.d.). Teaching Strategies for ADHD Students. Understood. https://www.understood.org/en/school-learning/partnering-with-childs-school/instructional-strategies/teaching-strategies-for-adhd-students

Understood. (n.d.). Building a Support Community for Your Child with Learning and Attention Issues. https://www.understood.org/articles/en/building-a-support-community-for-your-child-with-learning-and-attention-issues

Understood. (n.d.). How Kids with ADHD Can Learn to Manage Emotions. https://www.understood.org/articles/en/how-kids-with-adhd-can-learn-to-manage-emotions

Understood. (n.d.). Social Skills for ADHD: How to Help Your Child Make Friends. https://www.understood.org/en/learning-thinking-differences/child-learning-disabilities/add-adhd/social-skills-for-adhd-how-to-help-your-child-make-friends

WebMD. (n.d.). Exercise and ADHD: What You Need to Know. https://www.webmd.com/add-adhd/childhood-adhd/exercise-for-children-with-adhd#1

Printed in Great Britain
by Amazon